THE 100 DAY WAR

Also by Ray Henderson:

The History of the Pony Club

The 100 Day War

Copyright © 2013 by Ray Henderson.

All rights reserved. No part of this book may be used or reproduced in any manner without written permission from Lillium Press except in the case of brief quotations used in critical articles and reviews.

ISBN: 978-0-9628023-9-3

All colorized photographs from the Civil War done by Richard Downs ©.

Cover by Fred Finch Graphics.
WWW.fredricfinch.com.

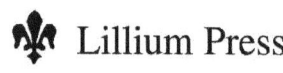 Lillium Press

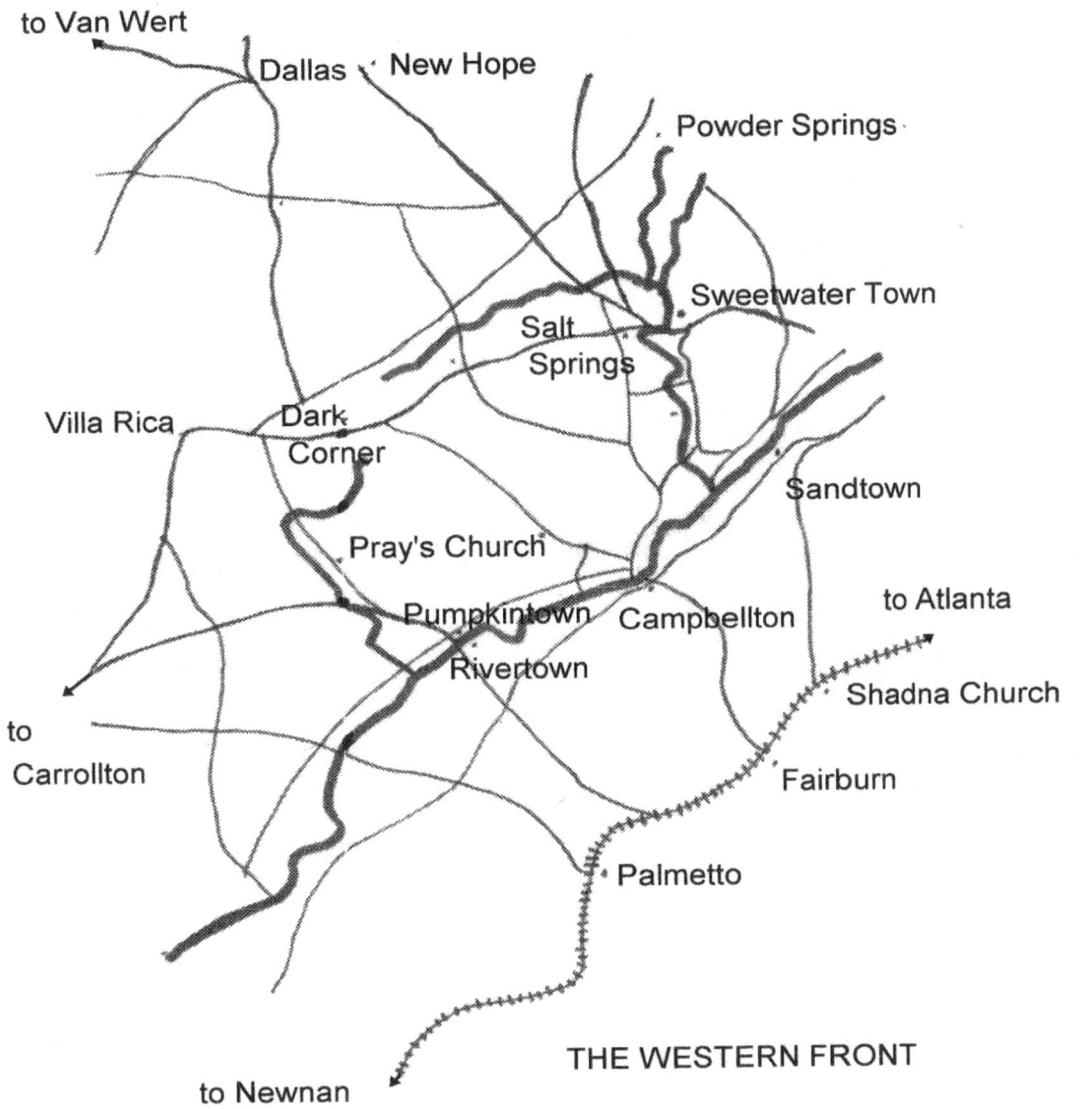

TABLE OF CONTENTS

GEOGRAPHY OF THE WESTERN FRONT	3
PREFACE: THE ACTORS	5
CHAPTER 1 JULY 1-5	12
OFFICIAL REPORTS	18
CHAPTER 2 JULY 5-15	33
OFFICIAL REPORTS	41
CHAPTER 3 JULY 15-AUGUST 3	60
OFFICIAL REPORTS	74
CHAPTER 4 AUGUST 3-SEPTEMBER 1	100
OFFICIAL REPORTS	104
CHAPTER 5 SEPTEMBER 1-OCTOBER 1	121
OFFICIAL REPORTS	126
CHAPTER 6 OCTOBER 1-NOVEMBER 11	152
OFFICIAL REPORTS	158

The following is a day by day account of the events of the Civil War along the Chattahoochee River west of Atlanta. The timeline begins June 29, 1864 and ends on November 11, when Atlanta was burned. The events described cover an area from what is now Cobb, Fulton, Douglas, Carroll, and Coweta counties. Campbell County in 1864 included what later became Douglas County and the southern part of Fulton County. Campbellton, on the Chattahoochee River, became the county seat in 1828 and represented the right flank of the Federal army arrayed against Atlanta. Campbell County sent 1500 of its population of 9,000 to fight against the northern aggression.

Included in the text are numerous maps. Day by day situation maps and maps used by both sides will be found. Pictures of locations, historic sites, artifacts and the people involved in the drama are reproduced to add life to the day to day activities of the armies.

To understand the cast of **Actors**, units and command structure are listed below:

UNION CAVALRY:
Cavalry Corps, Army of the Cumberland
Brigadier General Washington Elliot

1st **Division** commanded by Gen. Edward M. McCook

1st **Brigade**: Col. J. T. Croxton
8th Iowa Col. Joseph Dorr
4th Kentucky Mounted Infantry Col. John Croxton
2nd Michigan Maj. Leonidas Scranton
1st Tennessee Col. James Brownlow

2nd **Brigade**: Col. William Torrey
2nd Indiana Col. James Stewart
4th Indiana Col. Horace Lamson
1st Wisconsin Maj. Nathan Paine

Artillery:
18th Indiana Battery: Lt. W. L. Rippetoe

Gen. Edward M. McCook and Col. John T. Croxton

Cavalry Corps, Army of the Ohio
Major General George Stoneman
Col. Horace Capron
Col. Israel Garrard

1st Brigade: Col. Israel Garrard
7th Ohio Lt. Col. George Miner
9th Michigan Col. George Acker

2nd Brigade:
Col. James Biddle
Col. Thomas Butler
5th Indiana Col. Thomas Butler
6th Indiana Lt. Col. Courtland Matson

3rd Brigade: Col. Horace Capron
14th Illinois Lt. Colonel David Jenkins
8th Michigan Lt. Col. Elisha Mix

Adam's Kentucky Brigade:
Col. Silas Adams
1st Kentucky Maj. Frances Helveti
11th Kentucky Maj. William Boyle

Artillery (assigned 7-6-64):
24th Indiana Battery Capt. Alexander Hardy

After the Stoneman-McCook raid in late July, Sherman ordered Gen. Judson Kilpatrick to Replace McCook and Stoneman.

Gen. George Stoneman and Col. Silas Adams (color by Richard Downs©).

3rd Division:
Brig. Gen. Judson Kilpatrick

1st Brigade:
Lt Col. Robert Klein

Col. George Acker.

Col. James Biddle.

Maj. J. M. Young

3rd Indiana   Maj. Alfred Gaddis
5th Iowa Maj. Harland Baird

2nd Brigade: Lt. Col. Fielder Jones
8th Indiana   Maj. Thomas Herring
2nd Kentucky Maj. Owen Star
10th Ohio Lt. Col. Thomas Sanderson

3rd Brigade: Col. Eli Murray
Lt. Col. Robert King
92nd Illinois Mounted (9th cav.) Col. Smith Adkins
3rd Kentucky Lt. Col. Robert King
5th Kentucky col. Oliver Baldwin

Artillery: Capt. Yates Beebe
10th Wisconsin Battery

Gen. Judson Kilpatrick and Col. Eli Murray.

The confederate opposition remained constant throughout the campaign on the western flank of Johnston's and later Hood's army.

CONFEDERATE CAVALRY CORPS

Major General Joseph Wheeler

Jackson's Division:
Brig. Gen. William Jackson

Armstrong's Brigade:
Gen. Frank Armstrong
1st Mississippi Col. R. A. Pinson
2nd Mississippi Maj. John Perry
28th Mississippi Maj. Joshua McBee
Ballentine's Mississippi Regiment
Lt. Col. William Maxwell

Ferguson's Brigade:
Gen, Samuel Ferguson
2nd Alabama Lt. Col. J. Carpenter
56th Alabama Col. William Boyles
9th Mississippi Col. Horace Miller
11th Mississippi Col. William Inge
Scout Company (9th Miss.) Capt. Thomas Flournoy

Ross' Brigade:
Brig. Gen. Lawrence Sullivan Ross
1st Texas Legion (27th Texas) Lt. Col. John Brooks
3rd Texas Lt. Col. Giles Boggess
6th Texas Lt. Col. Peter Ross
9th Texas Lt. Col. Thomas Berry

Gens. Frank Armstrong Samuel Ferguson and Lawrence "sul" Ross.

Gen. Washington Elliott

Gen. Joseph Wheeler

Gen. William "Red" Jackson

Top left: Gen. Joseph E. Johnston, of the Army of Tenneessee, was replaced by Gen. John Bell Hood on July 17th, 1864.
General William T. Sherman, shown on horseback and in a Federal fort facing Atlanta.

The 1st Kentucky Cavalry (Federal): Col. Adams on the left, Capt. Wolford on right.

The 4th Kentucky Mounted Infantry AKA 4th Kentucky Cavalry.

Flag of the 55th Illinois Infantry.
General John Schofield.

CHAPTER 1 JULY 1 - 5TH

By June of 1864, Sherman's army had chased Joseph E. Johnston's Confederates from near Chattanooga to Kennesaw Mountain, just northwest of Atlanta. In a series of battles from Dalton to Resaca to New hope and Dallas, Johnston had successfully avoided being flanked and decimated. Now the Confederates were dug in on Kennesaw with no intention of leaving.

Sherman, having been repulsed several times in front of Kennesaw, once more began a flanking movement that would force Johnston's withdrawal and give the federals the Atlantic and Western railroad to the Chattahoochee River. His only supply line had to be extended to Atlanta's doorstep if his plans for taking the city were to be achieved.

Federal trenches facing Kennesaw Mountain, with Confederate trenches above them.

Sherman had a troop strength of nearly 109,000 before Kennesaw and sent cavalry under Gen. Stoneman south to cross Sweet Water Creek on the extreme left flank of the confederate Army. On July 1st, the cavalry crossed at Powder Springs Creek and entered old Campbell County. He passed Maroney's Mill (Sweet Water Road) and set up camp at the Maroney house at a place known as Cox's crossroads (corner of Highway 78 and Ben Hill Road). He sent scouts in all directions, while moving a force east toward the bridge at Sweet Water Town.

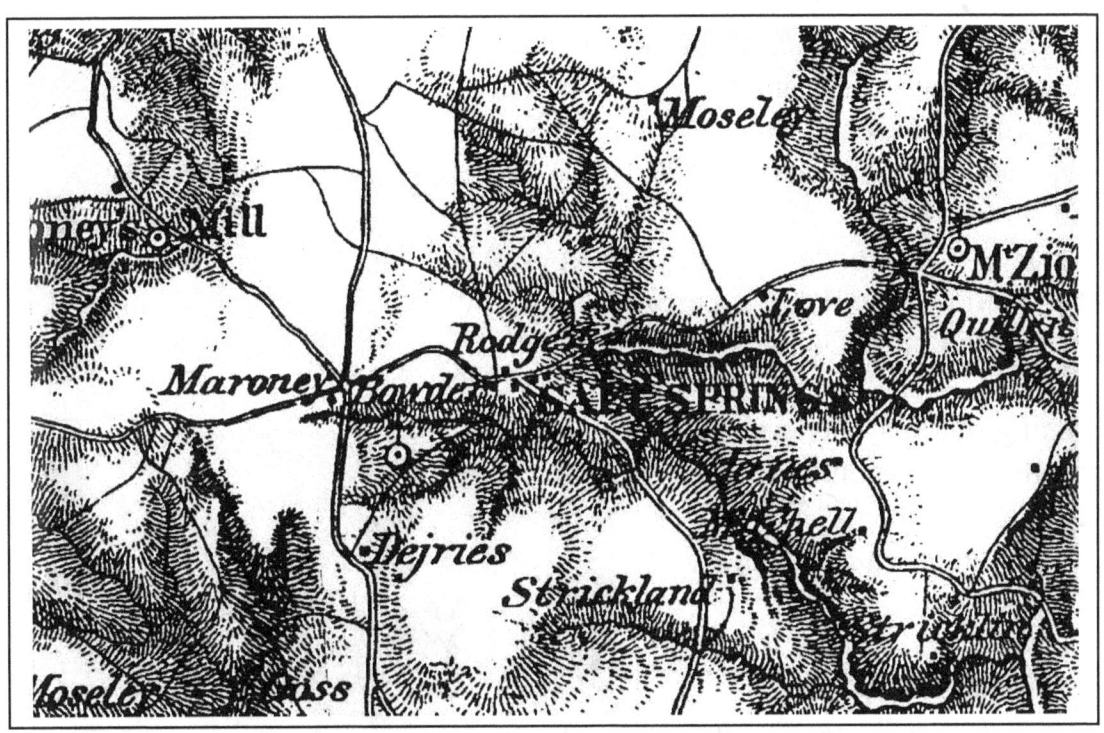

Stoneman took Cox's crossroads, the five road intersection at Salt Springs.

Stoneman believed there was a considerable force at Villa Rica, to his west and thought it imprudent to force a crossing at the bridge at Sweet Water Town. His forces went into camp at Bowden's and Maroney's.

On the 2nd, noting only a small force at Villa Rica, Stoneman fought his way across the bridge and secured Sweetwater Town. Here he would meet up with Schofield's infantry coming down the Powder Springs Road. He sent a scout down the Campbellton-Powder Springs Road to scout for a crossing over the Chattahoochee, and sent Col. Adams brigade down the west side of Sweet Water Creek to secure the bridge at Ferguson's Mill.

When Col. Adams arrived at the Sweet Water Factory, he immediately ordered the belting cut from the machinery and cloth pulled off the looms. The factory was shut down, the people rounded up and detained and his force settled into camp within site of the factory. By the end of the day, Stoneman controlled both bridges over the Sweet Water, the junction at Bowden's and that at Sweet Water Town. Camps were set up at Cox's Crossroads, the bridge at Sweet Water Town and the hill overlooking the factory at Tucker's Ford.

On the 3rd of July, Stoneman and McCook, with the help of the 55th Illinois infantry, under Gen. Schofield, began to advance on Confederate positions between Sweet Water Creek and the Chattahoochee River. Col. Capron was given command of the area around Sweet Water Bridge and Adams, with some of McCook's men began to sweep the east side of the creek toward the river. With one section of the 18th Indiana Battery, Adams left Ferguson's Bridge and met minor resistance at Alexander's Mill, from Capt. Alexander's 4th Ga. militia. They swept eastward down the Baker's Ferry Road until they were 300 yards from a Confederate trench (now Douglas Hill Road).

On the evening of the 3rd Federals lay siege to the works, bombarding it with parrot shells. The 3rd Texas Cavalry, in it's regimental history described the action:

Trench of State and Texas troops.

...On the third day of July we fought Gen. Schofield's nearly all day, fighting and falling back (as they were pushing down a road leading to Sand Town, a crossing on the Chattahoochee River), passing through a line of breastworks on the crest of a ridge crossing the road at right angles, erected and occupied by the Ga. Militia, about the middle of the afternoon. As we passed through the breastworks, one of our men was killed by a long range ball. The militia had never been under fire and had never seen a man killed before. We were

instructed to form a line immediately in their rear and rest; and to support them if the enemy should come, but beyond throwing a few shells over the works and skirmishing at long range, we had no further trouble with the enemy that afternoon...

Ross' Texas cavalry, meanwhile, was also covering the area below Sweet Water Town..They were falling back under pressure from both McCook and Stoneman's force and Schofield's 55th Illinois Infantry. By the end of the day, only Confederates at Ruff's Mill and the river kept Johnston's position at Kennesaw intact.

Saddle buckles, buttons, dropped Enfield and .44 rounds, sling border and piece of sabot from the trench on Douglas Hill Rd.

As July 4th dawned, the Federal threat continued. The 3rd Texas found itself under attack from Stoneman's and McCooks forces on the Baker's Ferry Road:

...The next morning the third went into these breastworks, and while Capt. Germany and myself were out in front deploying skirmishers he was severely wounded just below the knee and was unfit for duty for several months.

General Schofield's Corp advanced in a solid line of battle, and were allowed to take the works while we fell back a short distance into the timber and heard them give three cheers for Abe Lincoln, three cheers for Gen. Sherman and three cheers for Gen. Schofield. We then fought them again back through the timber until we came to a lane leading between farms across a little valley nearly a mile wide. On the hill beyond was our infantry in breastworks, and just beyond the breastworks was the narrow river bottom and Sandtown crossing, and down in this little bottom were our horses. As we entered the lane the enemy ran a battery up to the edge of the timber and shelled us every step of the way as we pulled through the long lane, tired and dusty, about noon that hot 4th of July. Passing

through the breastworks we mounted our horses in a shower of shells and crossed the river…

Case shot and .44 balls from the trench line guarding the Sandtown crossing.

Flag of the 3rd Texas Cavalry

By the end of the day, Stoneman held the river from the mouth of Sweet Water to the Sandtown crossing. He headquartered at Sweet Water Town, while Schofield settled in at the Gordon house, where the Sandtown and Howell's Ferry roads crossed.

For the past two days, Stoneman had sent scouts down to Campbellton to assess the crossing and the danger there. On the fourth, scouts clashed with Confederate forces. The **Regimental History** for the 1st Kentucky (Fed) Cavalry described the action:

On the 4th the enemy's cavalry crossed the river, fired upon our pickets, and companies D, I, J, K and L, with three companies of the 11th Kentucky pursued to the river at Campbellton, where a heavy skirmish took place, in which William Huff, of Company J, was killed…

The late **Rev. Henley Campbell** recounted this story through the years. The fallen Kentucky cavalryman was left in the care of Susan Bullard, whose house still sits on the banks of the Chattahoochee opposite the town of Campbellton. She was given instruction by the officer in charge to bury Pvt. Huff, respectably, or he would return and burn her house down. She complied, interring the soldier in her garden.

In 1994, while going through papers of the Kentucky Inspector General, at the State Archives, I came upon Huff's name as the only soldier killed that day. A later find was an entry in Capt. Wolford's diary, verifying the death of Huff. That summer, local historians and reenactors provided "boots and saddles" as a Veteran's Administration marker was consecrated for the former "unknown" soldier buried near the Bullard house.

| Marker for Pvt. William Huff. | The Bullard-Henley-Sprayberry House on Hiway 92. |

On the evening of July 4th, the Federals began to settle near the banks of the Chattahoochee River opposite Sandtown. Major camps were set up a mile or so from the river, to avoid shelling and to take advantage of the high ground overlooking all the ferry crossings on the river. These camps included a large force below Douglas Hill Road, near Camp Creek Parkway, to house pickets at the Sandtown Ferry and another on the Sandtown Road near the intersection of Old Thornton Road and Lower River Road. Smaller camps were located at the Cox' crossroads, Sweet Water Town, one in sight of Sweet Water Factory and one above Alexander's Mill.

THE OFFICIAL RECORDS JULY 1 – 5:

Hqtrs. First Cav. Div., Dept. of the Cumberland,
June 29 (30), 1864

General: I have the honor to report that a scouting party sent by me yesterday morning to Villa Rica, twenty two miles southwest of this point, has returned. They report that they found the country very thoroughly occupied by the enemy's scouts, so that they were compelled to take by roads and the woods for a great portion of the distance. There was no force either at Villa Rica or Pumpkinvine post office, but four brigades of the enemy's cavalry had been at Villa Rica day before yesterday, and marched from there in the direction of Sandtown. They report the country filled with scouting parties, and found a number of rebel soldiers hiding to escape these scouts. A party of sixty of the enemy passed through Villa Rica to Cedartown yesterday.

Very respectfully, your obedient servant,
E.M. McCook, Brigadier General, Commanding

Brig. Gen. W.L. Elliott,
Chief of Cavalry, Dept. of the Cumberland.

Headquarters Army of the Ohio,
July 1, 1864, 9:30 A.M.

Major-General Sherman:
Stoneman crossed the Sweet Water just below the mouth of Powder Springs Creek at 7 o'clock, and is pushing towards Sweet Water Town...

J.M. Schofield,
Major-General.

Hqtrs. Army of the Ohio
In the field July 1, 1864.

Major-General Sherman:
Stoneman reports the enemy's cavalry in strong force west of Sweet Water toward Villa Rica. He thinks it will not do to cross to the east of Sweet Water, leaving the enemy in his rear.

J.M. Schofield,
Major-General.

Hqtrs. Military Division of the Mississippi,
July 1, 1864.

General Schofield:
It is not reasonable to suppose Joe Johnston will keep at Villa Rica anything more than a cavalry force of observation. If Gen. Stoneman deems it impossible to occupy the position of Sweet Water Town, let him take position across Sweet Water Creek, below Powder Springs and put a regiment in observation near Salt Springs, on the road between Villa Rica and Sweet Water Town. The enemy's cavalry force will then be divided, and that is what I want.

W.T. Sherman,
Major-General, Commanding.

Schofield's Hqtrs.,
July 1, 1864-9p.m.

Major-General Sherman:
The line has been down, so that I could not communicate with you till now. I got your dispatches about the position you desired me to take and about Stoneman's movements. I found it necessary to go beyond Wade's about three quarters of a mile to get control of the roads. I have got the desired position and am entrenching securely. The Powder Springs Road comes in at Wade's; the Ruff's Mill Road branches off one quarter of a mile beyond Wade's, and intersects the Marietta Road at Moss', only a quarter of a mile from the Sandtown Road, on which we moved. The Marietta Road comes into the Sandtown Road only a half a mile from Moss', and three quarters of a mile from Wade's. (Gen.) Hascall holds all those crossroads, and his position is good. His artillery reaches the Nickajack, and his pickets are

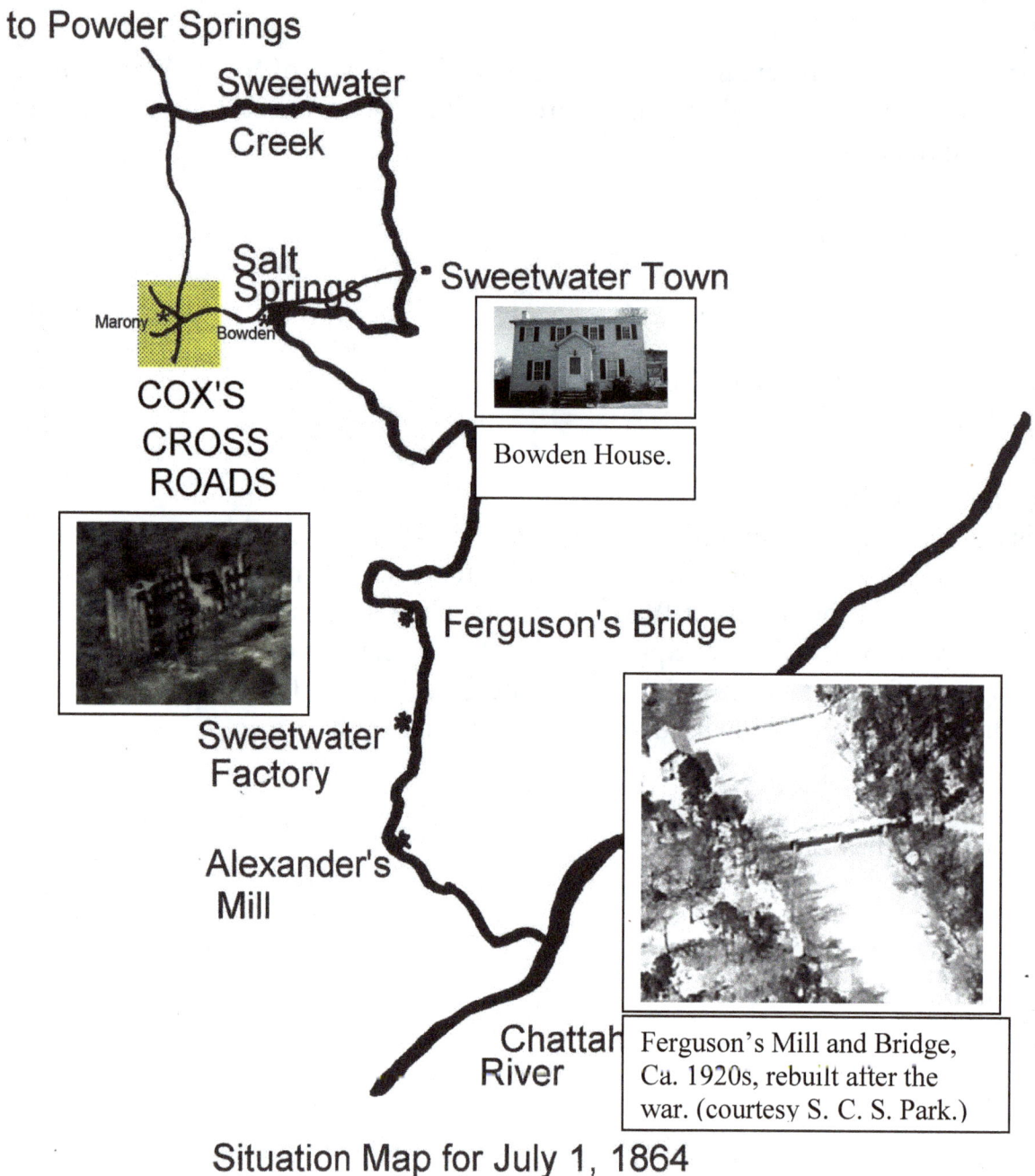

Situation Map for July 1, 1864

near it. The enemy seems to be in force beyond the Creek...Stoneman reports this evening that he has found only a small rebel force west of the Sweet Water. He sent a detachment to Sweet Water Town and found the bridge there strongly guarded. I will send him your instructions...

J.M. Schofield,

Major-General

Hqtrs. Army of the Ohio,
In the field, July 1, 1864-9p.m.

Maj.-Gen. George Stoneman,
Commanding Cavalry Corps, Dept. of the Ohio:
Gen.: I have received your dispatch of 6:15 p.m. I enclose one from Gen. Sherman, giving his views, etc...It occurs to me that you might, according to Gen. Sherman's plan, push a large force down this side of Sweet Water, and press the enemy back from the bridge at Sweet Water Town...

J.M.Schofield,
Major General, Commanding.

Hqtrs. Army of the Ohio,
In the field, July 2, 1864-12:50p.m.

Major-General Sherman:
The enemy is extremely quiet in my front and shows only a light skirmish line. At 10 o'clock Stoneman had possession of the bridge at Sweet Water Town and of the west bank of the creek as far down as the (Sweet Water) factory, with a force moving toward Campbellton. He was repairing the bridge and would push out on all roads to the north and east as soon as his horses could be got across. Stoneman has met no enemy except small parties. He thinks the main body of Jones' and Wheeler's cavalry is near Campbellton. His scouts just returned so report.

J.M. Schofield,
Major-General.

Sweet Water Bridge, July 2, 1864.
(Received 2p.m.)

General McCook:
We have a position that we can hold against the whole rebel army. Send up everything you have in the way of transportation, and everything there that may be

back at the bridge behind you belonging to my two brigades. Send and have the 100 men at the upper bridge and the 20 men at the ford below, where (Col.) Adams

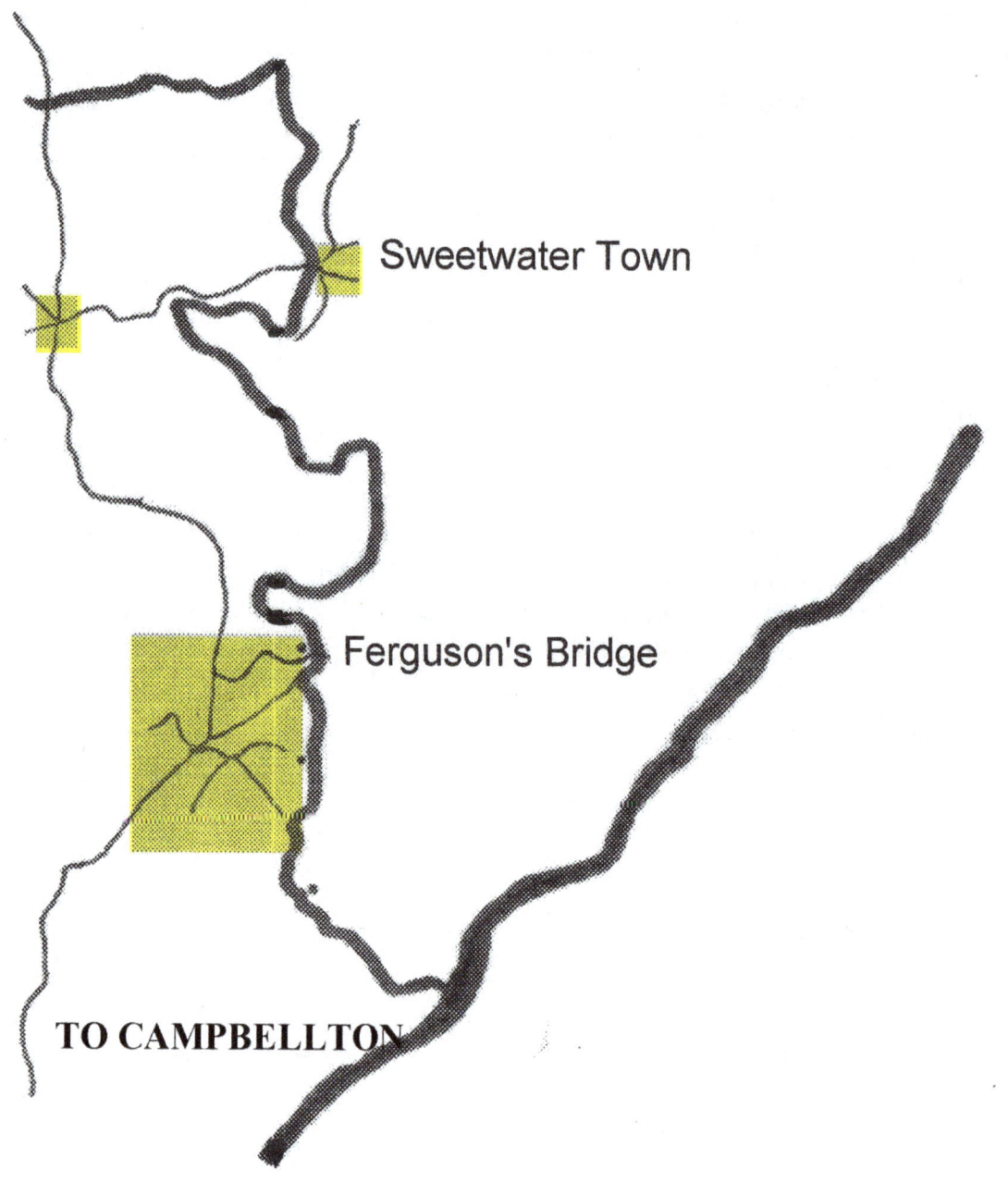

Situation Map July 2, 1864

Sweetwater Town

Ferguson's Bridge

TO CAMPBELLTON

crossed, relieved and sent to their regiments. After everything has passed by you send for Adams and come up yourself. I have opened up communications with (Gen.) Butler.

Stoneman,
General.

Tell Adams to have 100 men to hold the crossroads where you are now.
G.S.

July 2, 1864.

Gen. Schofield:
...Do you know whether McCook is with Stoneman? McCook has artillery; Stoneman, none.

W.T. Sherman,
Major-General.qtrs. Military Division of the Mississippi,
In the field, near Kennesaw, July 2, 1864.

Gen. Garrard, Commanding Cavalry:
...I will go to Cheney's or Wade's, down the Sandtown Road. Gen. Stoneman has been down to the Sweet Water Town and Factory, and controls that region.

W.T. Sherman,
Major-General, Commanding.

Hqtrs Army of the Ohio,
July 3, 1864-4 a.m.

Major-General Sherman:
I have heard from Stoneman. The force sent toward Campbellton returned, finding no enemy this side of Chattahoochee. All had crossed the river or Sweet Water Creek near its mouth, where there is a ford. Stoneman now holds a line from the

right of our infantry to Ferguson's Bridge, a little above Sweet Water Factory. McCook is at the bridge over Sweet Water on the Powder Springs and Campbellton Road...

J.M. Schofield,
Major-General

Hqtrs. Dept. and Army of the Tennessee,
In the field, Moss' House, Ruff's Mill Road,
July 3, 1864-2:30 p.m.

Major-General Sherman:
...Major-General Stoneman's cavalry, I understand, is on this side of Sweet Water, and is pushing east from Sweet Water Factory toward the Nickajack and Chattahoochee.

Jas. B. Mcpherson,
Major-General.

CSA Hqtrs. Ross' Brigade, Jackson's Cavalry Division,
In the field, Ga., July 3, 1864 - 9:20 a.m.

Brigadier Gen. Jackson, Commanding Division:
General: My scouts report the enemy with infantry and cavalry near Sweet Water Bridge, but could not ascertain their force. They think they camped there last night. The enemy in front of my position on the Sandtown Road remain quiet; no movements made by them this morning. I have made no change in my line, but have detached the Third Texas and sent them to guard the road, which my dispatch of yesterday informed you came into my rear.

I am, Gen., very respectfully. &c.,
L.S. Ross,
Brigadier General.

Hqtrs. Ross' Brigade, Jackson's Cavalry Division.
In the field, Ga., July 3, 1864 - 10:15 a.m.

Brigadier Gen. Jackson, Commanding Division:
General: A body of Yankee cavalry is now moving down the road on my left, one regiment, all that has been discovered. The skirmishers in my front are still advancing; are now but a little distance from my line.

L.S. Ross, Brigadier-General.

Hqtrs. Ross' Brigade, Jackson's Cavalry Division,
In the field, Ga., July 3, 1864 - 1:50 p.m.

Brigadier Gen. Jackson, Commanding Division:
General: The Yankee infantry is moving across my front in the direction of Sweet Water Bridge in front of Gen. Armstrong. Their line of skirmishers, which appears to be out merely for the protection of their flanks while moving, are in full view of my pickets, who report that their knapsacks are plainly visible. What amount of force is moving I cannot discover. You may be able to form some estimate of the force from the length of time they may be passing, which I will report as soon as it is done moving by.

L.S. Ross, Brigadier-General.

Hqtrs. Ross' Brigade, Jackson's Cavalry Division,
In the field, Ga., July 3, 1864 - 7:15 p.m.

Brigadier-Gen. Jackson, Commanding Division:
General: The enemy are advancing in my front once more with heavy line of skirmishers, before which my line is being slowly driven back. I cannot decide how large the force is in rear of the skirmish line, but it is at least a brigade of infantry. The line of skirmishers extends to my left beyond my farthest vedettes, and, I suppose, to Gen. Armstrong's front, as they can be heard that far. At this moment their advance is checked. My skirmishers are, however, not more than 100 yards in advance of my line.

Ross' brigade flag, 55th Illinois Infantry flag.

L.S. Ross, Brigadier-General.

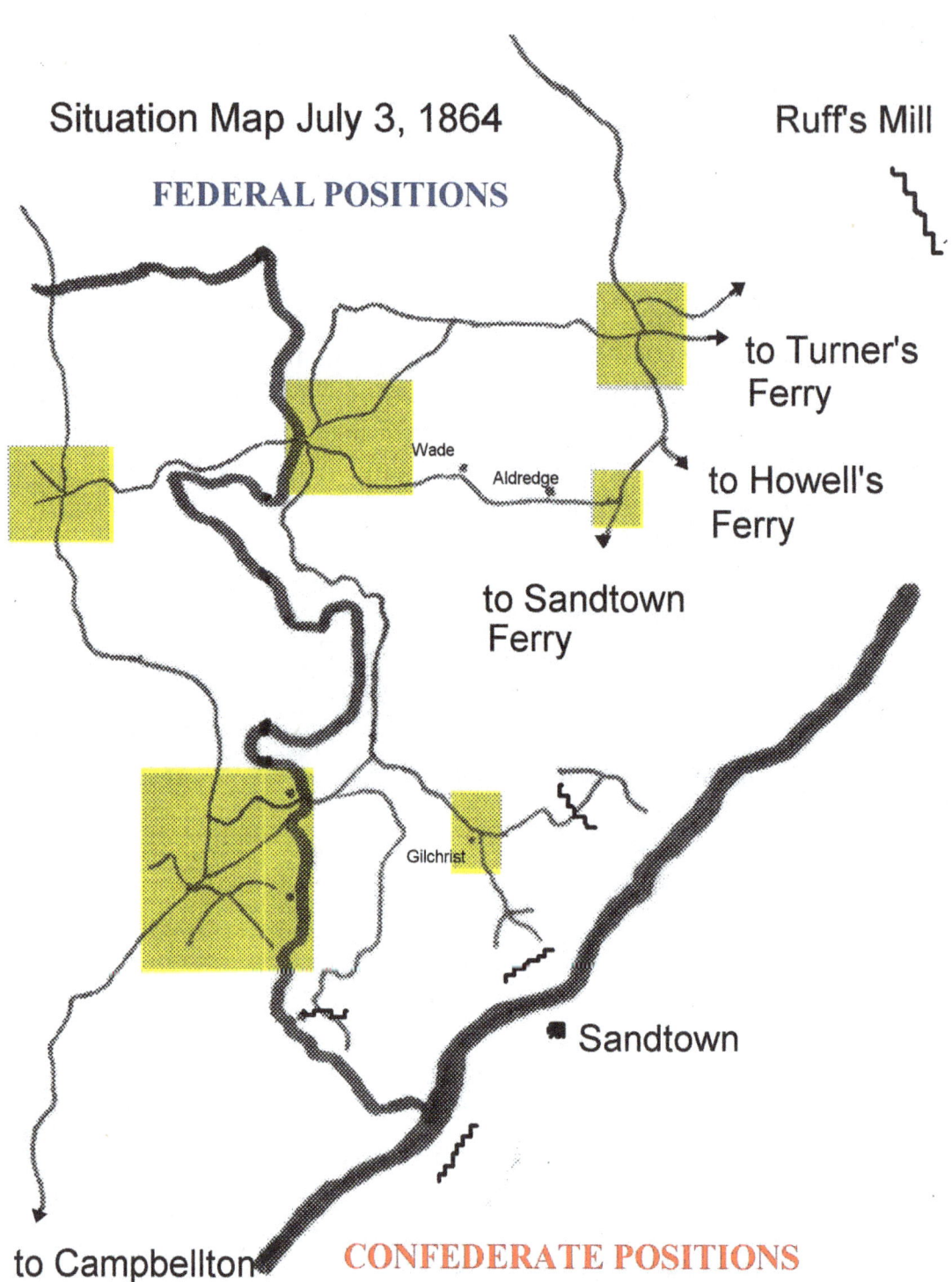

FED Hqtrs First Cavalry Division,
Near Sweet Water Creek, July 3, 1864.

General: I have the honor to report that my command has been operating under the orders of Gen. Stoneman since we left Lost Mountain. Our part, however, has been a secondary one. Found no enemy, except a few of Lee's Battalion State Militia. Col. Adams captured 4 or 5 of them, and one of my detachments, in a scout toward Pumpkin Vine, captured a Seargent and 2 men of Armstrong's scouts. No person in either of the commands has been killed or wounded yet. My impression is that the first day out we could have crossed the river at Campbellton or any place else near there...

E.M. McCook, Brigadier-Gen., Commanding.

Regimental Reports:

No. 396.
Report of Lieut. William B. Rippetoe,
Eighteenth Indiana Battery.
Hqtrs. Eighteenth Indiana Battery,

Sandtown, Ga. September 10, 1864.

Flag of the 18th Indiana Battery.

July 1, the command moved to Sweet Water Creek, below Ferguson"s Bridge. On the evening of the 3d of July two guns moved out on the Mason's Ferry Road, where they shelled the rebels, who were posted behind rail barricades, inflicting considerable damage...

Report of Capt. Cyrus M. Brown, Fifty-Fifth Illinois Infantry, of Operations from June 16 to September 5.
Hqtrs. Fifty-Fifth Reg. Illinois Infantry Vols.,
Camped near Lovejoy's Station, Ga., September 5, 1864.

July 2nd, the regiment, under command of Capt. Francis H. Shaw, marched eight miles to the right to support Gen. Schofield. July 3, they were engaged skirmishing with the enemy, driving their cavalry one mile from their front across Sweet Water Creek...

No. 390.
Report of Capt. Albert J. Morley, Fourth Indiana Cavalry.
Hqtrs. Fourth Indiana Cavalry,
Cartersville, Ga., September 6, 1864.

On 3d of July, brigade had an engagement with the enemy near the mouth of Sweet Water, in which the regiment participated...

No. 391.
Report of Capt. Lewis M.B. Smith, First Wisconsin Cavalry.
Hqtrs. First Wisconsin Cavalry.

Cartersville, Ga., September 6, 1864.
July 1, marched from Lost Mountain to Howell's Ferry (sic), on the Sweet Water.
July 3, sharp skirmishing with the enemy near the Chattahoochee River...

Hqtrs. Army of the Ohio,
July 4, 1864 - 7:45 p.m.

Capt. L.M. Dayton, Aide-de-Camp:
...Please inform the General that Stoneman's Cavalry has control of the country from McPherson's right, on the Turner's Ferry Road, to the river near Sandtown. He has beaten the enemy's cavalry in several small affairs and captured many prisoners and a large number of good horses and mules...

J.M. Schofield, Major-General.

In the field, July 4, 1864 - 8 a.m.

Major-General W.T. Sherman,
Commanding Military Division of the Mississippi:

...Stoneman's cavalry hold the country from the Sandtown Road west to Sweet Water, and most of his cavalry is along the Sandtown Road...

Jas. B. McPherson, Major-General.

Regimental Report No. 296.
Report of Major-Gen. John M. Schofield, U.S. Army, Commanding Army of the Ohio.
Hqtrs. Army of the Ohio,
In the field, Decatur, Ga., September 10, 1864.

During the 1st, Gen. Stoneman, supported by Gen. McCook, crossed the Sweet Water with a portion of his cavalry, and moved down the south bank to gain, if possible, the crossing near Sweet Water Factory, and threaten the Chattahoochee at Campbellton. One brigade (Adams') was left to cover Hascall's right during this advance. Stoneman met no enemy south of the creek, except a few small parties of cavalry, but found the bridge at Sweet Water Town partially destroyed and strongly guarded. He was, therefore, unable to secure the crossing that day. The next morning he crossed without difficulty, only a battalion of militia having been left to watch the crossing, and also reached the river opposite Campbellton with but slight opposition. Our infantry right was now at a point five miles in rear of enemy's left, ten miles from the key of his position - Kennesaw - and only four miles from his railroad and six from the Chattahoochee, while we controlled the Sandtown Road to the river. The position seemed exposed and the movement to gain it hazardous, yet when once gained and entrenched it was really secure, for the enemy could not detach force enough to dislodge us without abandoning his position about Kennesaw and hazarding a general engagement in open field...

CSA Mason's and Turner's Ferry,
East bank, July 4, 1864.

(Gen. Joseph E. Johnston:)
General: The following are the ferries and crossings between this point and Gorman's Ferry, twelve miles southwest:
Green's (private) Ferry: A mile and a half southwest of this point. Hill on west side command the ferry; ferry not fortified or guarded, and ferry boat still there.

Green and Howell's Ferry: Three miles Southwest of this point. Ferry fortified on east side; redan with one piece of artillery, and rifle pits for 100 or 150 men. Two companies (seventy-five men) guard the ferry boat on east side river.

Howell's (old) Ferry (now disused): One mile southwest of Green and Howell's, is fordable in dry weather. Ferry not fortified or guarded. No ferry boat at this point now.

Wilson and Baker's Ferry: Three miles southwest of Green and Howell's; fortified on east side for 100 men.

Sandtown: Two miles southwest from Wilson and Baker's; fortified on east side by rifle pits for 100 or 150 men. Ferry boat on east side of river.

Adaholt's (sic): Two miles southwest from Sandtown Ferry; fortified on east bank of river, with rifle pits for 100 or 150 men.

Gorman's: Two miles south of Sandtown; fortified on east side and guarded by one company.

At most, if not all, the ferries mentioned above as now in use the ascent and descent to and from the river on either side is good for artillery or wagons. The highest ground and most commanding positions for artillery, in my judgement, are found on the west bank of the river - that is the bank from Atlanta. On our (the east) side, in some instances, pretty fair positions for artillery a little back from the river can be obtained.

Brigadier-General Hume's division of cavalry (two brigades) has just passed down the river for the purpose of reinforcing the State troops at the crossings mentioned above. I have furnished the commanding officer with a guide and all information I had. On yesterday evening at 4 o'clock the enemy were moving bodies of infantry, number not known, to and around Sweet Water Factory. A portion of this cavalry, evidently on a reconnaissance, appeared opposite to Adaholt's Ferry, but on being fired upon by the State troops retired.

W. Clare, Major and Asst. Inspector-General.

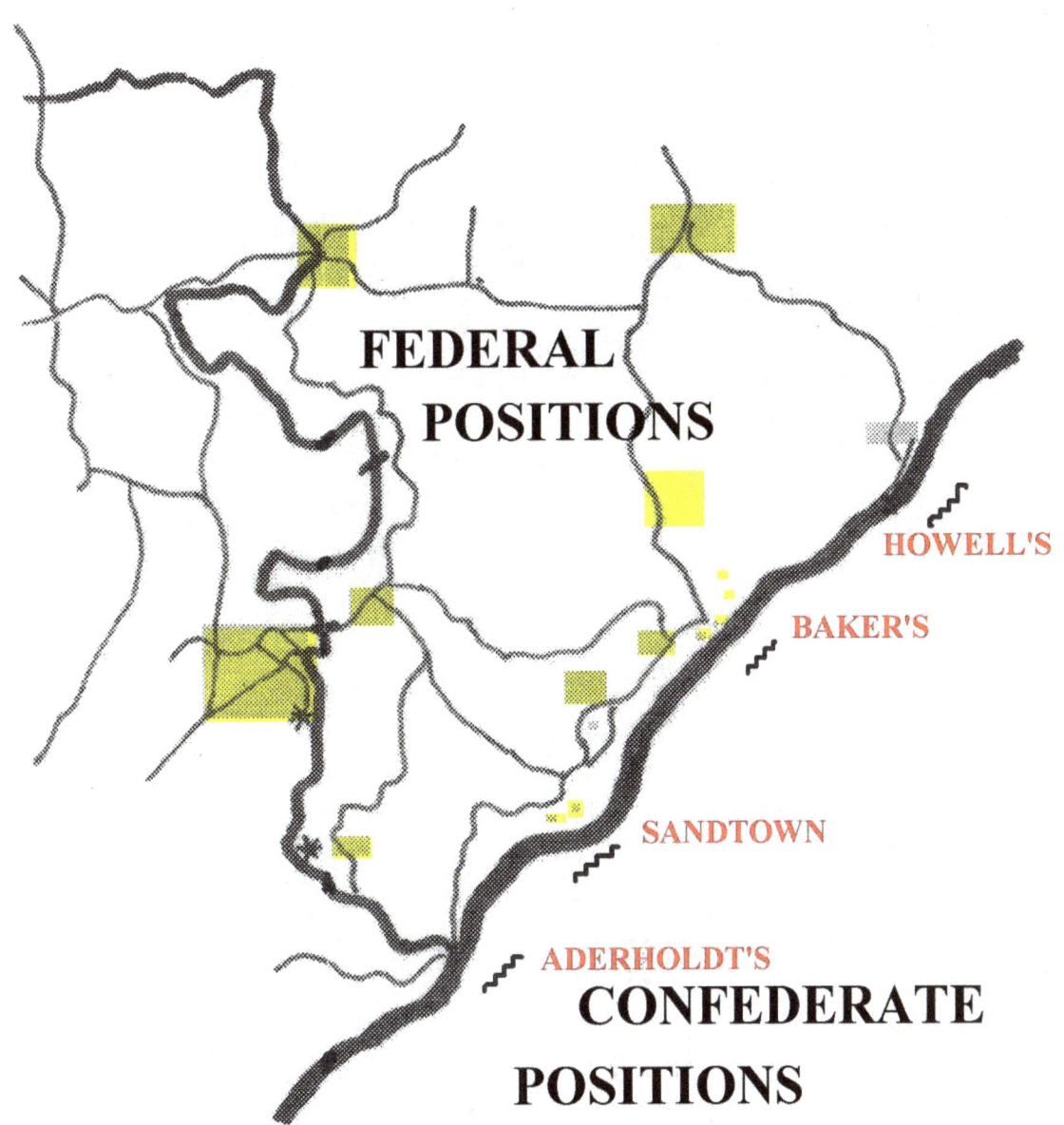

The Flat Rock School, replaced by this community center, where the 30th Georgia, Company C (later G) signed up for duty in the Civil War. It was later used as a hospital as Hood's troops marched to Allatoona in September and October, 1864. An adjacent cemetery includes Confederate dead.

The Summerlin-Bowden House, on Hiway 78, built c. 1840 as a stagecoach inn, and where 41st Ga. Co. K signed up.

CHAPTER 2 JULY 5 - 15

As soon as the Confederate army pulled out of the area between Carnpbellton and the Sandtown Ferry, the civilian population began to move. This was described in an unpublished manuscript (1929) by Helen Bagget, who lived a few miles from where Douglasville is now. In her voluminous work, in the possession of the Old Campbell County Historic Society, she described the scene as people refugeed to Campbellton to cross the river:

Well, by and by, when all the rebels crossed over the Chattahoochee, refugees began to come from the sections north of us, follering (sic) the side roads, seeking the main road to Campbellton Ferry. When I reached the road, it was a sight to behold. A long, unending line of refugees stretched the length of the road, either way, as far as the eye could see.

She saw horse, and ox drawn wagons with people and possessions in them and people carrying things on foot as well. Herds of cattle, horses and pigs accompanied those souls seeking safety on the other side of the river.

People's possessions were in great peril in those times and they brought all they could carry and left, buried, at home, other family treasures. Helen Bagget wore all

Refugees prepare to leave before the armies arrive.

five of her best dresses as she and her horse approached the ferry. No one wanted to stay in the occupied area and all feared for their land and homes left behind.

General Halleck would later justify Federal actions in occupied areas in a letter to Sherman:

Not only are you justified by the laws and usages of war in removing these people, but I think it was your duty to your own army to do so. Moreover, I am fully of the opinion that the nature of your position, the character of the war, the conduct of the enemy, and especially of noncombatants and women of the territory, which we have heretofore conquered and occupied, will justify you in gathering up all the forage and provisions which your army may require, both for a siege of Atlanta and for your supply in your march farther into the enemy's country. Let the disloyal families of the country thus stripped go to their husbands, fathers and natural protectors in the Rebel ranks. I approve of taking or destroying whatever may serve as supplies to us or the enemy's army (9-28-64).

Foraging got out of hand and there are many tales of Federal actions resulting in pillaging houses. In a letter to Colonel R.N. Adams from General Corse, the latter excoriates the former for pillaging:

Colonel: in riding through the camps this morning, I was very much grieved to find, in the Twelfth illinois Infantry, lying shamelessly exposed to the whole command, a lot of male and female clothing and wearing apparel, shirts, bed quilts, &, evidently recently pillaged from some of the neighboring helpless citizens (9-5-64).

Further, there is the story of the Summerlin cemetery, across from the Bowden House on Highway 78: Joseph Summerlin died in 1860 and was buried in a metal casket with a glass top, so that his grandson could see him as he grew up. Federal bummers broke the glass and removed the ring from the deceased man's hand.

The best source of data for these activities comes from the Southern Claims Commissions, records at the Federal Archives. The Claims Commission served but a short time, handing out Millions of dollars to those whose possessions were confiscated by Federal Armies. Here in the South, little of what was taken was accounted for at the end of the war. One such family was that of Miles G. Mosely, who was visited by Col. Adams of the Kentucky Cavalry and by other units, starting on July 2 and ending ten days later. Troops took the following:
6 year old mule $ 175.00
corn 12 bu.   12.00

wheat 75 bu.   112.00
pork 75 lbs.   10.50
beef 200 lbs   18.00
oats 50 bu.   50.00
bacon 50 lbs   10.00
1 2 horse wagon   60.00
 total claim: $448.50

His father, Isaah Mosely, entertained 600 troopers carrying 3 regimental flags, on the 5th and 6th. He lost his corn, wheat, oats, his bacon, sheep and hogs. He complained to Stoneman's headquarters in Salt Springs, but was told to go home.

Nelson Tucker was a Union man all the way. Though he had two sons in the Confederate Army, his third served as a driver of an ammunition wagon for the Federals, his daughter married a member of Co. D 25th Illinois after the war and Nelson accompanied Federal Cavalry to show them crossings on streams and rivers. He farmed 950 acres near the intersection of 1-20 and Camp Creek

Sgt. James Carrol, of the 25th Illinois, Co. D, married Elizabeth Tucker in 1865.

Parkway, a nearby stream which fed into the Sweetwater, is still called "Tucker's Branch". Federals took his oats, corn, potatoes and wheat, as well as his 60 head of hogs, 2 mules and a plowing mare. His $ 535.00 claim was payed by the Federals after the war.

Many others living in Salt Springs, near Campbellton or along the river also made claims. They include: 3 of the Aderholds; John Busby, Israel Causey, Ben Cooper, Harrison Coursey, 2 Demoneys, John M. Edge, Tom Giles, Ann Hilderbrand, Levi Holloway, John Humphries, Celia Joiner, John Kennedy, Mary Mitchell, Hillery Moates, Wiley Padgett, Ben Rogers, Nancy Stewart, Roswell Strickland, Aaron Turner, J.P. Watson, Ebenezer White, E.R Whitley and 2 Winns.

Almost from the begining of the Atlanta Campaign, it became evident that the civilian population was to bear the onus of guilt in the eyes of the Federal armies. Sherman's great weakness was his extended supply line and he was constantly vigilant for those who would disrupt it. Both armies relied heavily on the railroad system, both desired to get behind the other to break the road and take victory. Having taken the area above the Chattahoochee River, the Federal army stared at the Confederates on the other side, over the flowing no man's land, each thinking of how one could get behind the other. Sherman greatly distrusted the population in his rear, fearing their calumny could tilt the balance to the enemy.

Sherman excersized Special Order #10, ordering Stoneman on July 5th "...*try and pickup as many of his (rebel) scouts as you can and gather in as prisoners every citizen of whom you entertain a suspicion.*" General Whipple had several citizens of Dallas, Ga. arrested and "*banished from the United States (7-11-64)*". On July 14th, Sherman clarified his policy:

Everything in the nature of grain, forage and vegetables should be collected. No suspicious persons or citizens should be allowed near the railroad or in the country. The safety of this army must not be imperiled by citizens. If you entertain a bare suspicion against any family, send it North. Any loafer or suspicious person seen at any time should be imprisoned and sent off. If guerrillas trouble the road or wires between Kingston and Acworth, they should be shot without mercy ...

Sherman did have people arrested throughout the campaign and many were either sent North or to South America. The best example of the former is the fate of the Roswell and New Manchester Factory employees. On July 2nd, Col. Adams of the 1st Kentucky Cavalry occupied the town of New Manchester and its cotton factory. The Federals immediately destroyed the belting to stop the factory from producing cloth for Confederate uniforms. The townspeople were detained for several days, until Sherman ordered them arrested and sent north of the Ohio River. Major Thompkins and a detachment of the 14th Illinois Cavalry arrived on the 9th to torch the factory. Henry Lovern, in charge of the factory, in deposition (1868), explains:

When Major Thompkins got to the factory, he said that he had burnt the Roswell Factory on Thursday, previous, and that he had orders from Gen. Sherman to burn this factory, and he intended to do it. And he said the hands must fix up to go West, where they could get provisions, so they intended to destroy everything in that part of the country, to prevent the enemy's scouts from troubling their men.

Aerial photo of the ruins of the Sweet Water Factory.

Opinions on the fate of the Sweet Water operatives differ. Some, like Sophie Irvin, watched the factory burn, then walked home to Salt Springs. Others were given the opportunity to sign an oath of allegiance and go home. Those who refused were picked up by wagons on the 10th, sent to The Georgia Military Institute at Marietta, where they were put on trains to Louisville, Ky. Those who signed the oath were set free, north of the Ohio River, the rest were incarcerated for the duration of the war. Many died in the prison camp, or from the journey back to Georgia. Many children were orphaned, relatives later scouring the North after the war in attempts to find them. The majority of women with children sent north never returned, but men and those who owned land in Campbell County did find their way home. This whole episode resulted not only in hardships for these families, but for their men in the Confederate Army. As soon as local companies found out what was happening, they began to desert, crossing the Chattahoochee to follow their families. In Co. C, 30th Ga., 22 men deserted after July 4th, many accompanying their families on the train ride north.

Gov. Morton of Indiana was not impressed with Sherman's policy: "*Large numbers of Southern refugees, women and children, entirely destitute, are coming here, filling the depots and streets. Our citizens are doing everything for their relief (12-28-64)...*".

Civilian mill operatives under guard at the Ga. Mil. Institute.

Two of the Causey girls, sent to Indiana as children by Sherman. (courtesy of Russel Mosely.)

GHOST AT NEW MANCHESTER

In the mill race of Sweetwater Factory is a 1,000 lb flat stone, wrenched from the shoals and placed at the spillway. When the creek is up from rains and the millrace swells with rushing water, the large stone bounces up and down in a rhythmic fashion. Old timers swear it is the heartbeat of one of the young lady operatives who still awaits her sweethearts return from the dangers of war.

Meanwhile, the Federal Cavalry continued to consolidate its position on the river from Buzzard's Roost to Campbellton. The lst Kentucky Cavalry, Federal, in its regimental history, indicates this process:

July 6th: at 2pm. scouted Campbellton, had a lively skirmish, drove the enemy back into its camp and retired to a camp near the river.

July 7th: Regiment ordered back to near Powder Springs, while Cos. J and I remained 4 miles behind to guard a bridge over Sweetwater Creek

July 8th: Returned to former camp near Sweetwater Creek.

Union command was hearing almost daily reports of Confederates crossing the river to get behind the Federals, but Sherman was spending a great deal of his time planning to cross the Chattahoochee at various points. His efforts included a raid on the railroad west of Atlanta. To achieve this, he sent Stoneman's Brigade toward Carrollton, on July 11th. He advised Gen. Halleck in Washington:

1 have also three points at which to cross the Chattahoochee in my possession and only await Stoneman's return from a trip down river, to cross the army in force and move on Atlanta. ...(7-17-64) .

The Moore's Bridge Raid required all of Stoneman's 3500 men. In their absence, Sherman ordered Gen. Blair to picket the river in place of Cavalry. Blair soon found out that this was no picnic and increased his pickets to include every hill overlooking the river. In the archeological record, strategic hills show carbine bullets dropped and Smith and .58 "three ringers" present, while other hills have only Infantry bullets present. The long range of Infantry rifles finally offset the Confederate advantage over short range carbines along the river front.

The raid began July 12th, the regiments taking different routes, to cut off all Confederate scouts and surprise the enemy at Moore's Bridge, between Carrollton and Newnan. The majority followed the Atlanta-Villa Rica Road and then south down Liberty Road, as it is now called. When they reached the bridge, they surprised the Tennessee Confederate Cavalry, who were guarding the bridge. Stoneman took the bridge and rifle pits on the opposite bank, but sudden reinforcements caused the Federals to recross and burn it. On the return trip, the brigade spent the night at Skint Chestnut, on Sweetwater Creek and along the Atlanta-Villa Rica Road, before returning to camp on the Sandtown Road

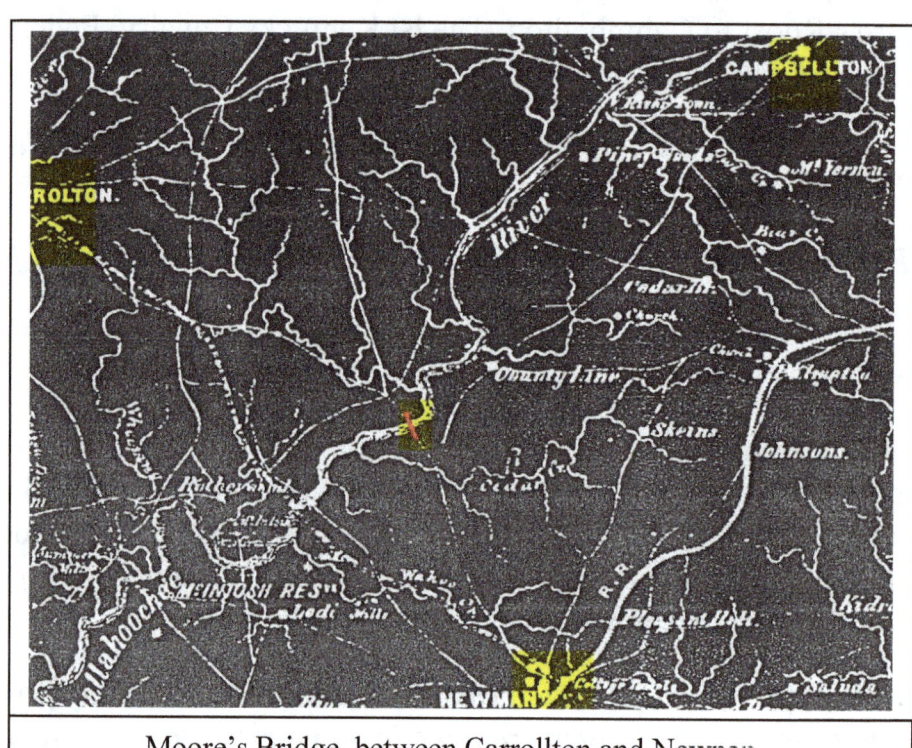

Moore's Bridge, between Carrollton and Newnan.

OFFICIAL REPORTS: July 5 - 15th

Sandtown Ferry, Ga., July 5, 1864

Major-General Sherman:
General: I think or at least hope that during the past six or seven days we have accomplished all that was expected of us; if not, it has not been from (lack of) efforts to do so. We have worked day and night and have covered a good deal of country. I was detained on the 1st by representations from Gen. McCook to the effect that a few days before a large cavalry force had been in Villa Rica, and the correctness of which I was forced to ascertain by sending out strong scouting parties, and also to see where the force had gone to. I found that the force had been a good deal magnified, and that it had either gone south of the Chattahoochee River or across the Sweet Water near its mouth, where there is a good ford and the only one on the Creek...I have now one brigade at Baker's Ferry, one at and below Sandtown, and a third in reserve.....

If Barry has a good four-gun battery, I could make use of it, as I have a lot of dismounted men I could make use of to support it. We have all the transportation we want and can move at any time, with twenty days' supply for the men. All we lack is ammunition for some of our arms, and that I am told is not to be obtained. Gen. McCook informs me that he is in the same fix. I wish I could get my regiment, or rather the regiment to which I belong (the Fourth [Kentucky Mounted Infantry]), with us. Can't you manage it?
I enclose a sketch of this region (see below).

George Stoneman
Major-General, Commanding

July 6, 1864-9:30 p.m.

Gen. McPherson:
Your note of this 5 p.m. confirms my impression that there has been for the past forty-eight hours an extensive movement of the enemy down the river. Trains of wagons have been seen during the day and heard during the night-time moving rapidly down the river, and long columns of cavalry have been seen and heard. Every prominent point on the other side has a redoubt and rifle-pits, which effectively prevent us from getting near the river. I however got close enough today to see it in three places, and found it not so wide as I expected. The bottoms

are very narrow and the ground gently sloping down on each side. This side is much more open than the other, the woods approaching the stream only in a very few places, and we were shelled whenever we came out into the fields in any force, so that we have to stay with the animals a mile or two back from the river in the woods. They have all the scows and canoes on their side, and well guarded by men behind rifle-pits armed with guns of much longer range than our carbines. The negroes that came across the river last night say that Wheeler with "his company" passed down the river yesterday and last night, and with the heavy smokes back from the river opposite the mouth of Sweet Water indicate no inconsiderate force in that region. The negroes say that the troops were going down to keep us from crossing at Campbellton, or in that vicinity, and that they are throwing up works all along the river. I have myself seen them at work in many places and at all the crossings. I am now covering upwards of twelve miles of the river with pickets and scouts. I have not yet heard from the scout I sent down to Campbellton. I have also guards at all the crossings on the road from Powder Springs to Campbellton. The country, with the exception of a skirt on the river and creek, is densely timbered and quite broken. Please transmit the information herein contained, or such portion as may be interesting to know, to Gen. Sherman, as he desires me to keep him informed and advised.

Stoneman, General.

Hqtrs. Military Division of the Mississippi,
In the field, near Chattahoochee, July 7, 1864.

Gen. Garrard, Roswell, Ga.: ....I repeat my orders that you arrest all people, male and female, connected with those factories, no matter what the clamor, and let them foot it, under guard, to Marietta, whence I will send them by cars to the north. Destroy and make the same disposition of all mills save small flouring mills manifestly for local use, but all saw mills and factories dispose of effectually, and useful laborers, excused by reason of their skill as manufacturers from conscription, are as much prisoners as if armed. The poor women will make a howl. Let them take along their children and clothing, providing they have the means of hauling or you can spare them. We will retain them until they can reach a country where they can live in peace and security...

W.T. Sherman,
Major-General, Commanding.

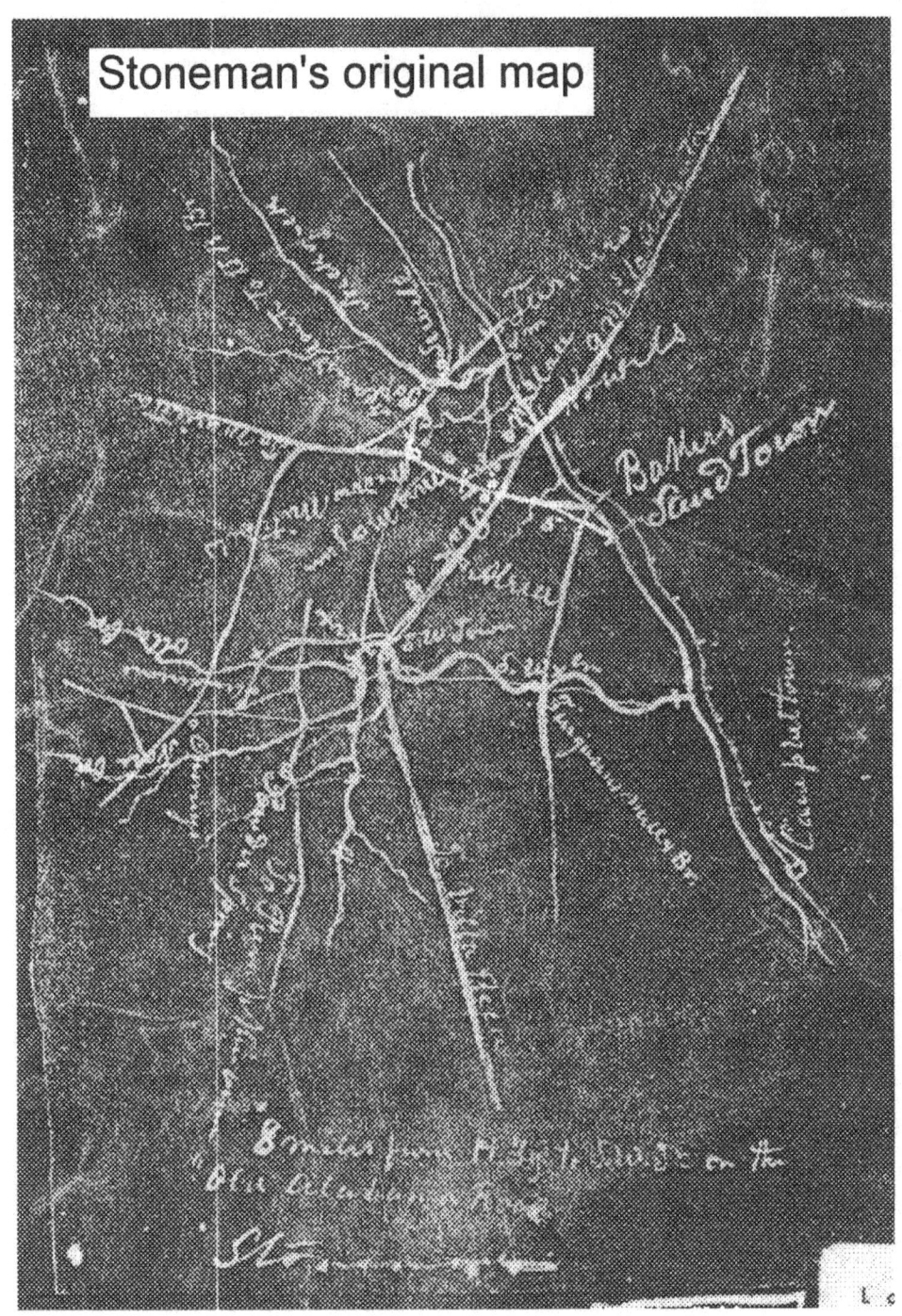

Hqtrs. Cavalry Corps,
July 7, 1864 -10:30 p.m.

Colonel Capron, Commanding Brigade:

I sent you an order by your staff officer to move down to Sandtown Ferry. Circumstances render it necessary to change your location, and I wish you would move by the Alabama Road to-night in time to reach Sweet Water Town bridge (the point you occupied a few days ago) by daylight tomorrow morning. Your pickets along the river will be relieved by the infantry tomorrow morning, after which they can join you. Col. Adams, who is a few miles below where you will be on Sweet Water Creek, thinks the enemy is in considerable force is on this side of the Chattahoochee River, and west of Sweet Water Creek. I wish you would push Scouting parties well out on the Alabama Road toward Villa Rica, and at the same time to Powder Springs, going by the bridge over the Sweet Water Creek (upper one [Gothard's]) over which we passed, and returning via the bridge over Noyes' Creek over which we passed, and around to the right. Pick up all scouting parties you can and arrest all suspicious persons. You and Col. Adams act in concert, and have an understanding with each other in regard to all movements. I will try to be with you tomorrow, if I can get through with Gen. Sherman in time. Keep me advised of what you see, hear, and do, and oblige.

Stoneman, General.

In the field, July 7, 1864 - 12 m.
Major-Gen. G.M. Dodge,
Commanding Left Wing, Sixteenth Army Corps:

Enclosed I send a copy of dispatch just received from Major-Gen. Sherman. From it you will see that he wants us to keep our troops well in hand for any movement, but at the same time make demonstrations as though we were trying to find a crossing on the Chattahoochee. The enemy have batteries of from one to four guns opposite all the ferries as near as I can learn, and are strengthening their defenses, and the banks on the opposite side from us are lined with sharpshooters. I wish you could take or cause a regiment of infantry and a section of artillery to go to each of the ferries (Howell's and Sandtown). Let a portion of each regiment be deployed as sharpshooters to disturb the enemy, and open on his batteries or any train or column of troops you may see moving. Major- Gen. Stoneman reports that the enemy have been moving troops and trains down the river for the last twenty-four hours. I send Capt. Reese down with this order, who will accompany the regiments and artillery as he is familiar with the roads, &c.

James B. McPherson,
Major-General.

  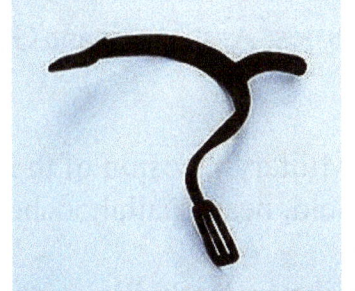

| Federal saddle shield from camp opposite Sandtown. | Federal stirrup from camp north of Baker's Ferry. (courtesy: Mike Gill) | Federal spur from Baker's Ferry picket posts. (courtesy: Scott Fields) |

Hqtrs. Dept. and Army of the Tennessee,
In the field, near Chattahoochee River, Ga., July 7, 1864.

Maj.-Gen. G.M. Dodge,
Commanding Left Wing, Sixteenth Army Corps:
General: In order to relieve a portion of Major-Gen. Stoneman's cavalry, so that he can make a scout to the west of Sweet Water Creek, as well as to keep up appearances of trying to find a place to cross the Chattahoochee, you will send one brigade of your command at an early hour tomorrow morning down to the vicinity of Sandtown Ferry, where the Sixty-Sixth Illinois is at Present, and have them extend their pickets down the river about one mile to a hill just below Lawyer Edge's house.

James B. McPherson,
Major-Gen., Commanding.

Hqtrs. Left Wing, Sixteenth Army Corps,
In the field, Ga., July 7, 1864

Brig.-Gen. T.W. Sweeny,
Commanding 2d Division:
Send one regiment of infantry (sharpshooters) to the river at Sandtown Ferry. Have the infantry engage the rebel Skirmishers on the opposite side of the river and gain the river if possible. Send one section of artillery with the regiment to cooperate

with it. Capt. Reese, of Gen. McPherson's staff, will accompany them. Make a determined effort as though you were going to cross. Use artillery freely.
By order of Maj.-Gen. G.M. Dodge:

J.W. Barnes, Asst. Adjutant-General.

Hqtrs. Military Division of the Mississippi,
In the field, near Chattahoochee River, July 9, 1864.

Gen. Webster, Nashville:
I have ordered the arrest of the operators at the Confederate Manufactories at Roswell and Sweet Water, to be sent north. When they reach Nashville have them sent across the Ohio River and turned loose to earn a living where they won't do us any harm. If any of the principals seem to you dangerous, you may order them imprisoned for a time. The men were exempt from conscription by reason of their skill, but the women were simply laborers that must be removed from this district.

W.T. Sherman,
Major-Gen., Commanding

Hqtrs. Military Division of the Mississippi,
In the field, July 9, 1864.

Gen. McPherson,
Army of the Tennessee:
General: ...Johnston sees I threaten Decatur and Stone Mountain, and now is a good time for Stoneman to strike south. I want him if possible to secure a point at Campbellton or below, and strike the West Point Road. I do believe he can do it, for Johnston will spread his force so much that it will be weak at all points. I have told Stoneman that if he secures both banks at Campbellton, with its ferry boats, he may call on you for a brigade to hold it whilst he strikes the railroad...

W.T. Sherman.
Major-Gen., Commanding

Hqtrs. Military Division of the Mississippi,

Near Chattahoochee, July 9, 1864.

Major-Gen. Stoneman, Commanding Division of Cavalry:
General: In pursuance of our conversation of this day, I have to request that you proceed with your command to Campbellton tomorrow night, Appearing suddenly before the place and securing if possible the boats there, or forcing the enemy to destroy them. If you can possible do it get possession of those boats and also of the other bank. I am very anxious that an attack or demonstration be made against the railroad below Atlanta, and will instruct Gen. McPherson to have a brigade of infantry ready to come down and hold the river whilst you with your cavalry strike the railroad. I am satisfied that the crossing of Schofield and Garrard above will draw in that direction Johnston's chief army, and that what troops are left south of Atlanta will be strung out as far as West Point, where he will keep the chief force. The point where the road would be easiest reached will be, say half way from Atlanta and West Point, but it would not be safe for you to pass Campbellton, unless the ferry was well destroyed. A ford but little known or used below Campbellton and this side of Franklin bridge will be the best if such exists, and you may incur any risk sure of my approval, for whether you make a break of the road or merely cause a diversion you will do good. Don't be absent more than four or five days, and keep me advised on all possible occasions.

W.T. Sherman,
Major-Gen., Commanding.

Hqtrs. Dept. and Army of the Tennessee,
Near Turner's Ferry, July 10, 1864 - 12m.

Major-Gen. Sherman,
Commanding, &c:
General: ...Major-General Stoneman is here, and desires to know whether the retreat of the rebels across the Chattahoochee will make any change in the plans proposed for him yesterday. If he goes on the expedition, he wishes to start at 8 o'clock this evening. From the result of his reconnaissance last night in the vicinity of Campbellton, he finds there is no bridge or ford until he reaches Franklin, and no enemy on this side of the river. I send this by Capt Gile in order to get an answer quickly.

James B. McPherson,
Major-Gen.

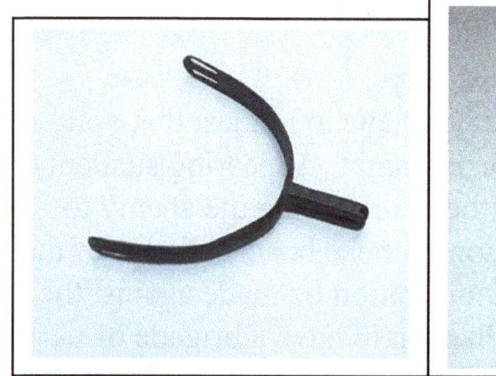 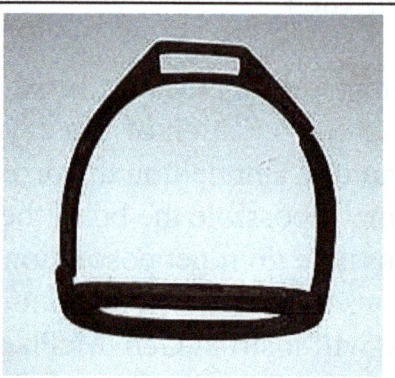 

| Confederate spur from Sandtown Road. (courtesy: Scott Fields) | Confederate Stirrup from Baker's Ferry. (courtesy: Mike Gill) | Confederate saddle buckle from Jones' Ferry on Sweet Water Creek. |

Hqtrs, Dept. and Army of the Tennessee,
Near Chattahoochee River, Ga., July10, 1864 - 10 p.m.

Major-Gen. W.T. Sherman,
Commanding, &c:
General: Major-Gen. Stoneman has made all his arrangements and started on his expedition at 8 o'clock this evening, intending to go as far down as Campbellton tonight...Major-Gen. Stoneman said that he did not care about the infantry covering the river any farther down than the mouth of Sweet Water. If he cannot effect a crossing in the vicinity of Campbellton, he will, after making a lively demonstration there tomorrow, push rapidly tomorrow night for Franklin Bridge and try to cross there.

James B. McPherson,
Major-Gen.

Hqtrs. Dept. and Army of the Tennessee,
Near Chattahoochee, July 10, 1864 - 1:30 p.m.

Major-Gen. F.P. Blair, Jr.,
Commanding Seventeenth Army Corps:
General: Major-Gen. Sherman has directed Gen. Stoneman with his cavalry to move down the river to Campbellton, or below, and, if possible, to get across the river and cut the railroad between Montgomery and Atlanta. To do this will require

his whole force. You will, therefore, direct Gen. Leggett to send one of his brigades down immediately to a point in the vicinity of Sandtown Ferry to picket and guard the river at Howell's, Baker's, Sandtown, and Adaholt's (sometimes called Dodge's) Ferries, taking the place of the cavalry pickets. The infantry will march light, and anything required for them can be sent down tomorrow. The infantry are to guard the line of the river down as far as the mouth of Sweet Water Creek until the return of the cavalry expedition.

James B. McPherson,
Major-Gen.

Hqtrs. Dept. and Army of the Tennessee;
In the field, July 11, 1864 - 7:45 p.m.

Maj.-Gen. W.T. Sherman,
Commanding, &c.:
General: ...One brigade of Leggett's Division is near Sandtown Ferry picketing the river, and I have one brigade of Morgan L. Smith's Division near Widow Mitchell's, and the other brigade at the intersection of the Sandtown and Alabama Roads. Tomorrow morning De Gress will take his battery of 20 pounder Parrots, and go down to Sandtown Ferry and try to knock a small battery of the enemy's on the south side of the river to pieces. Gen. Stoneman got off last night. No news from him today.

Gen. Frank Blair.

Jas. B. McPherson,
Major-Gen.

CSA
General Field Order no. 3,
Hqtrs. Army of Tennessee,
July 11, 1864.

Intercourse between the pickets of the enemy and our own is strictly and positively prohibited. Officers of all grades are required to watch over the enforcement of this order and to punish every infraction. Gen. Johnston appeals to the good sense of the army to put an end to a practice so dangerous. Yesterday the enemy had a great interest in finding the fords in the Chattahoochee and easily attained their object, the pickets by mutual agreement bathing in the river together. The engineers of the enemy most probably mingle with the bathers.
By command of Gen. Johnston:

A.P. Mason,
Asst. Adjutant-Gen.

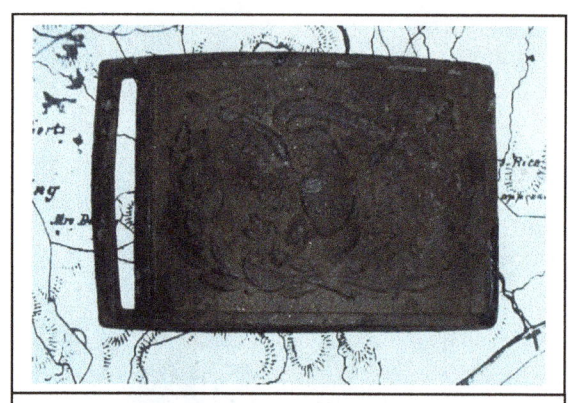

Federal sword belt plate from near Campbellton.

Federal canteen from road to Gorman's Ferry.
(courtesy: Mike Gill)

Hqtrs. Third Division, Seventeenth Army Corps,
Turner's Ferry, July 12, 1864.

Lieut. Col. A.J. Alexander, Asst. Adjutant-Gen.:
Colonel: During the day we have done all in our power to extend our information as to the character and number of the enemy in our front. The Forty-First Mississippi is opposite us near the mouth of the Nickajack; the Thirty-Second Georgia is opposite to us at Howell's Ferry, with what supports, if any, I do not know. Stewart's Division of Hood's Corps, is opposed to us in the region of Sandtown Ferry. A band of guerillas, consisting of Georgia State Troops, was on this side of the Chattahoochee, just beyond the Sweet Water, last night. Stoneman

was near Campbellton this morning, not having effected a crossing. He reports the enemy, 8,000 strong, opposing him.

M.D. Leggett,
Brigadier-Gen.

Moore's Bridge, Ga.,
July 13, 1864

Major-Gen. Sherman,
Commanding Military Division of the Mississippi:
General: By taking a roundabout way, and by unfrequented roads, our parties succeeded in capturing or cutting off every scout the enemy had out. We surprised the guard at the bridge (the First Tennessee Cavalry), and we drove them from the bridge before they had time to set fire to the straw and pine knots prepared for its conflagration. The Eleventh Kentucky Cavalry had the advance, under Col. Adams, and did the thing handsomely. The bridge had been partially destroyed by tearing up the sleepers and planks, but we will have it repaired during the night. It is a covered structure, very well built, 480 feet long on two spans. One of the couriers we captured came down on this side of the river, bore a message to the commanding officer here that the Yankees were coming in large force, and that he must hold the bridge at all hazards, and that re-enforcements were on the way. This point is twenty-five miles from Campbellton. There is another bridge at Franklin, twenty-five miles lower down. Newnan, on the railroad, is ten miles from here, and I understand the road leads through dense woods. We will try what we can do tomorrow morning as soon as it is light. I can hear of no railroad bridge in this vicinity. The people, negroes and others, say the road runs on a ridge, but if we do nothing to the road it will create a diversion.

George Stoneman,
Major-Gen.

Hqtrs. Seventeenth Army Corps,
Near Chattahoochee River, July 13, 1864.

Major-Gen. Sherman,
Commanding Military Division of the Mississippi:

General: ...The enemy have at various points along the river small boats in which parties can be conveyed across at night, making it necessary to have heavier pickets than would otherwise be required, which accounts for the fact the reserve is so small.

Frank P. Blair, Jr.,
Major-Gen., Commanding.

Hqtrs. First Brig., Third Div., 17th Army Corps,
July 13, 1864.

Capt. J.C. Douglass, Asst. Adjutant-Gen.:
Captain: I have the honor to report that all remains quiet here. The rebels appear to have a continuous picket-line along the river; none on this side. At regular crossings and where ravines go down to the river they have earthworks. I have seen only two embrasures and they are without guns. Yesterday afternoon one gun opened near Sandtown Ferry on men in a blackberry patch, and another on a reconnoitering party which went to Adaholt's Ferry, at the mouth of Sweet Water. They were brought up and taken away by the rebels; were not in position. About 2 o'clock yesterday afternoon, a body of cavalry - some of the pickets call it one, some two regiments - accompanied by four or five wagons, went toward the interior from Sandtown Ferry. A body of infantry - they called it a brigade - accompanied by about thirty wagons, moved to the south of southwest, from near the same point. They can be seen only a short distance from the river, however. Opposite Adaholt's, clothes hanging on bushes indicate a small camp. In a valley between Baker's and Sandtown Ferries, perhaps Utoy Creek, has appeared to be a larger camp, judging by smoke and the glimmer of fire. Nothing heard down the river, except two guns about dusk in direction of Gen. Stoneman.

M.F. Force,
Brigadier-Gen., Commanding Brigade.

Hqtrs. Seventeenth Army Corps,
Near Chattahoochee River, July 13, 1864.

Brig.-Gen. M.D. Leggett,
Commanding Third Division, Seventeenth Army Corps.

General: A report from Gen. Stoneman to Gen. Sherman says that he made an effort to cross at Campbellton, but from the condition of the river and the position of the enemy was unable to do so. He, however, left one brigade there, and has gone on to Franklin with the remainder of his command. In an endorsement upon this paper Gen. Sherman directs that a picket be kept "at the ford across Sweet Water near its mouth, the same that is used by the cavalry." The Major-Gen., Commanding, desires you to carry this order into effect by placing a strong picket at the point indicated, keeping up your line along the river.

A.J. Alexander,
Asst. Adjutant-Gen.

CSA
Atlanta, July 13, 1864 - 1p.m.

His Excellency Jefferson Davis:
The enemy are reported by Gen. Wheeler as having crossed two Corps this side of the river about nine miles above the railroad bridge. An official report has just reached Gen. Wright that the enemy's cavalry, accompanied by artillery, crossed the Chattahoochee this evening nine miles from Newnan. We're at last accounts advancing on that place. Our army is sadly depleted, and now reports 10,000 less than the return of 10th June. I find but little encouraging.

B. Bragg.

Atlanta, July 13, 1864.

Gen. S. Cooper:
Brigadier-Gen. Jackson commands three brigades, which are severally under Brigadier-Gens. Armstrong, Ferguson and Ross. Effective total, 3,574. Total present, 5,370.

J.E. Johnston.

Moore's Bridge, July 14, 1864.
(via Newnan).

Gen. Mackall:
I arrived here at 4 a.m. Found the enemy in possession of the bridge where Gen. Humes' pickets had been surprised. I have a small portion of my brigade; ordered the remainder to follow. I think I can hold them in check until my troops get up. They are working on the bridge. The abutment was knocked down. They have an excellent position and have made breastworks. It is a division of cavalry, with artillery. I have heard of no infantry. Scouts report a cavalry column gone below.

Frank C. Armstrong,
Brigadier-Gen.

FED
Hqtrs. Military Division of the Mississippi,
In the field, near Chattahoochee River,
July 15, 1864.

Gen. Thomas:
I have heard from Gen. Stoneman. He attempted to cross at Moore's Bridge, but encountered too much artillery, and thought it imprudent to attempt, lest he might not get back. He is now near Villa Rica, and will move this evening to Sweet Water. I have ordered him to come on over to Turner's Ferry and relieve Gen. Blair, whom I have ordered to draw out of sight of the enemy tonight and move tomorrow for Roswell...

W.T. Sherman,
Major-Gen., Commanding.

Camp near Villa Rica,
July 15, 1864.

Major-Gen. Sherman:
General: As I indicated to you in my last note, we completed the bridge (Moore's), and were ready to cross at daybreak yesterday morning, but before we essayed it a report came from Major Buck, in command of a battalion seven miles above, that the enemy had been crossing above him on a boat or a bridge, and that his pickets had been cut off. I, of course, made preparations accordingly, and found that the report originated in the sound made by the enemy crossing a bridge over a creek on the other side of the river, and nearly opposite to Major Buck. On attempting to cross the bridge the enemy opened upon it with four pieces of artillery from the

edge of the timbers on the opposite side and made an endeavor to retake their rifle-pits near the water's edge. Deeming it expedient to push our endeavors further, and knowing that it was easier to retain the men long enough to burn the bridge than to get them back again after they had been driven off, I ordered the bridge to be burned and the boats that had been collected there for security destroyed. During the day I sent scouts down the river to within thirteen miles of Franklin, where there is another bridge, and found neither fords nor ferry boats, and in the evening came to this point. We shall remain here and graze during the day, and in the evening move to the vicinity of Sweet Water Town, or within eight miles of it Col. Biddle, who was left with his brigade at Campbellton, reports the enemy quite strong at that point, with two guns of long range in each of two redoubts on the opposite bluff, which are opened upon him whenever any of his men show themselves. We get plenty of forage for the horses, beef, and blackberries, and some bacon for the men, and are getting on finely. We want horseshoes and nails, and a little time where we can avail ourselves of a blacksmith shop to fit the shoes, to complete the cavalry and make it ready for any service. The artillery, however, want better horses and better ammunition, as the horses they have would be unable to make long consecutive marches, and the ammunition is but little better than solid-shot. I was very anxious to strike the railroad from personal as well as other considerations, but I became convinced that to attempt it would incur risk inadequate to the results, and unless we could hold the bridge, as well as penetrate into the country, the risk of capture or dispersion, with loss of animals (as I could hear of no ford), was almost certain. It is impossible to move without every step we take being known, women as well as men acting as scouts and messengers. I have sent to the rear about 40 prisoners, 1 of them the commander of the picket at the bridge on this side, and 16 or 17 of them pickets and scouts in the vicinity of the bridge. I am unable to say how much force is opposite to us, but from what can be seen and I can hear, I am convinced it is no inconsiderable one.

George Stoneman,
Major-Gen., &c.

Flag of the 14th Illinois Cavalry.

FEDERAL ACTIVITY IN CARROLLTON AND VILLA RICA

As early as June 29th, Federal cavalry had been scouting Vlla Rica and the extreme left flank of the fight for Atlanta. On July 7th, the 8th Michigan had a sharp skirmish with Confederate scouts at Dark Corner and Federal scouts had been down toward the river to Whitesburg. Here, the William Amos Factory complex was first seen. Amos immediately began to disassemble the machinery for a train ride to Spartanburg, S. Carolina (where it was last reported as burning with that train). When Federals showed up on the 21st of July, William Amos, himself, was shot while refugeeing with the machinery (case 9281, trustees vs. Brumby and Russell, May 15, 1867).

During the Moore's Bridge Raid, Major Buck of the 8th Michigan was given the task of securing Stoneman's left flank. His diary states :

July 14, Broke camp at 10 o'clock - marched 12 miles - went on to scout Phillip's Ferry - marched from there to Moore's Bridge - and back to the ferry that night.

July 15th, recieved from Gen. Stoneman orders to establish a courier line thru from Moore's Bridge to Carrollton and to report to Gen. Stoneman every hour - it took me all day to get it thru paths.

July 16, marched 23 miles to Carrollton at night - arrived there at 3 am - stayed there all day and night.

In David Evan's *Sherman's Horsemen*, he picks up the story:

He left Major Buck, his reputation somewhat tarnished after the false alarm at Phillips' Ferry, and a small detachment of the 8th Michigan to keep an eye on the Rebels across the river and scout as far west as Carrollton before rejoining the rest of the command. Quitting the river about 3:00 P.M. on July 14, Buck and his men apparently marched leisurely. It was daylight the next morning before they covered the fifteen miles to Carrollton.
   The townspeople had little or no warning of their approach. Some bolted for the woods. Others simply stood and gawked at the dust-covered horsemen plodding down the street.
   "It was really pitiful to watch the terrified countenances of the women when our boys went into their houses to procure water or food," noted a Michigan soldier. "They seemed to think that we were ferocious wild beasts seeking whom

we might devour. But a few polite gentlemanly remarks from our boys, or a few winning smiles would dispell [sic] the illusion and before they left the house, the dear chivalrous ladies would become quite sociable and acknowledge that they had been deceived by their own men in regard to our ferociousness." A spontaneous, if somewhat forced, effusion of Southern hospitality followed and soon Major Buck and his men were feasting on the best Carrollton had to offer. "I have heard a great deal about Southern beauties," added the Michigan trooper, "but have been unable to find them when compared with our own Northern girls. What they call beauty here would be considered North as very commonplace."

After eating their fill, Buck's men strolled into several stores, where they discovered "heaps of tobacco." It had been a long time between chaws for most of them, and after appropriating all the tobacco they could carry, they destroyed what was left and took whatever else struck their fancy. "The town, except those houses which were still inhabited, was completely sacked," noted Samuel Tobey, the 8th Michigan's assistant surgeon?

About noon, a small detachment of the 14th Illinois rode into town with orders for Major Buck to remain in Carrollton until the next morning then catch up with the rest of the command at Sweetwater Town. Their message delivered, the Illinois boys rode on, part of a larger force Stoneman had sent out that morning with instructions to sweep the roads to the southwest, confiscating all the horses and mules they could find...

...Major Buck's battalion of the 8th Michigan also moved east on July 16. After spending the night bivouacked in a vacant lot in the center of Carrollton that would later become the site of the Carroll County courthouse, they broke open a few boxes of tobacco they had previously overlooked and then rode out of town, taking at least one unhappy Confederate with them. Traveling leisurely on the Old Alabama Road, they halted for the night about six miles west of the bridge at Sweetwater Town. The next afternoon, they caught up with Horace Capron's brigade, which had left Mitchell's Crossroads about 1:00 P.M. with orders to picket the Chattahoochee from Nickajack Creek down to Howell's Ferry.

In the Regimental History of the 1st Mississippi Cavalry Lt.Col. Frank Montgomery reports the Confederate response to the Moore's Bridge Raid:

We were not quiet long in our command, as will be seen from this extract from General Johnston's report. "On the 14th, a division of federal cavalry crossed the river by Moore's bridge near Newnan, but was driven back by Armstrong's brigade, sent by Brigadier General Jackson to meet it." Newnan is about forty miles southwest of Atlanta on the railroad leading to West Point, and the enemy's object was to cut this road, of the last importance to us while we could hold Atlanta. We made a forced march and succeeded in intercepting them before they reached the railroad, and though they had a division, we drove them back across the river with but little loss to us, and not much, though some, to them. We destroyed this bridge, and General Armstrong remained in the vicinity of Newnan a few days observing them, and waiting for orders.

Lt. Col. Frank Montgomery.

Mississippi I button and part of Memphis Novelty Works spur. From sites opposite Campbellton.

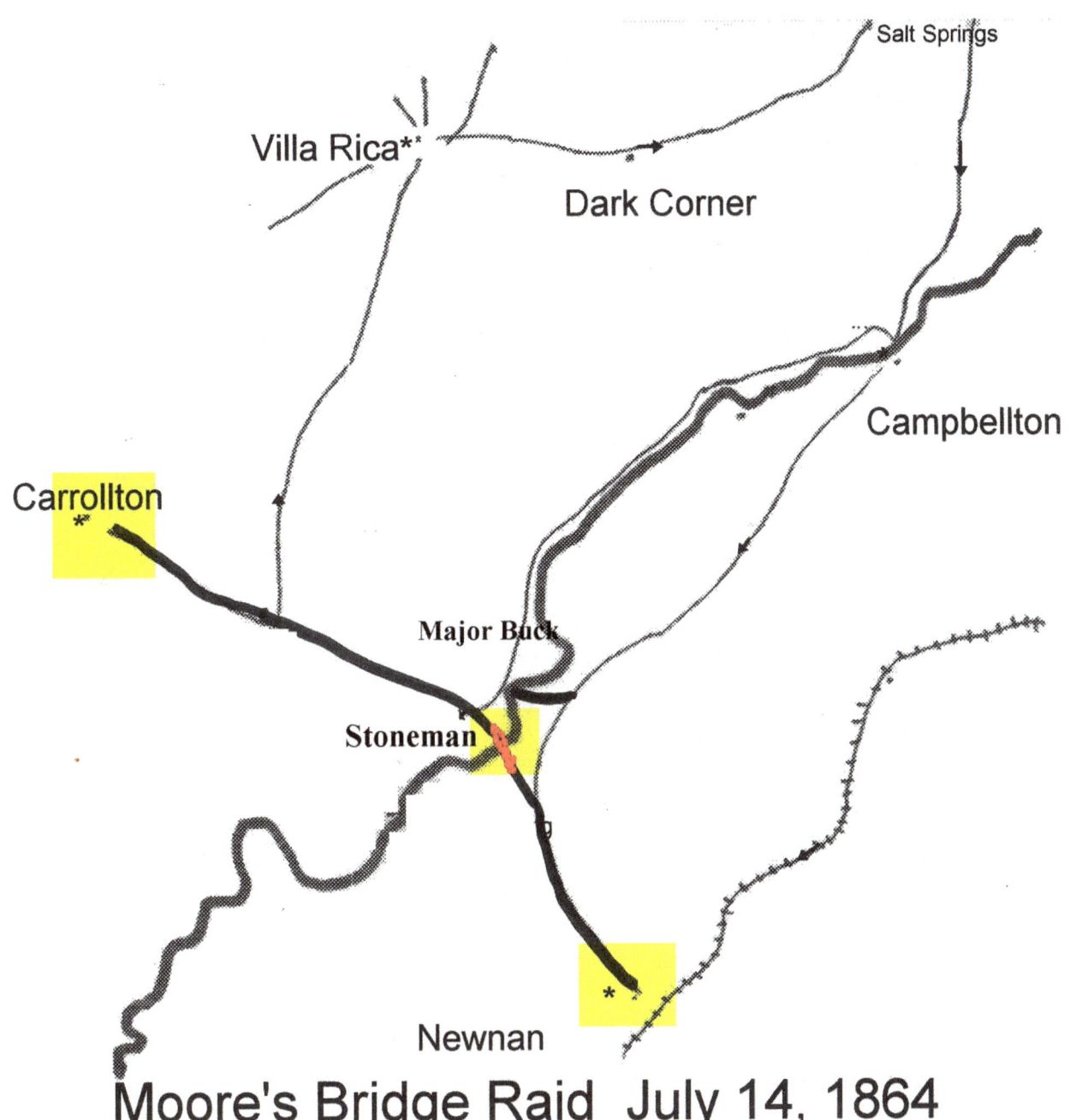

Moore's Bridge Raid   July 14, 1864

CHAPTER 3 JULY15 - AUGUST 3

ISAIAH LOVE'S VIEW OF THE CIVIL WAR AT SANDTOWN FERRY

There is an interesting story about the effect of the shelling on the civilians across from Sandtown. In a house built in 1867, not far from here, lives the granddaughter of one of David K. Love's slaves. Isaiah Love was a slave of Absolom Baker, the operator of Baker's Ferry, located between Interstate 20 and Camp Creek Parkway. Absolom Baker's daughter, Mary Catherine, married David K. Love in 1861. Isaiah, a slave and part of her dowry, came to work on the Love Plantation and found himself on the river opposite Sandtown when the cannon duels began. Like many of the others there, he was so frightened by the noise that he decided to take his family, some of the stock and other needful things and seek shelter in the rock overhangs on nearby Sweetwater Creek.

Isaiah and family had been gone only a few days when the slave superintendent showed up with tracking dogs. The canine patrol found them all in a deep recess near the top of a steep ridge. The superintendent called for them to come down and return to the plantation, but Isaiah would have none of that. As the superintendent and his barking posse ascended the slope, Isaiah sent a shower of embers from his cook fire down on the approaching host. This was enough to force a hasty retreat by the patrol. His luck held out as the search party failed to return and was not heard from again.

After two weeks of living like a troglidite, Isaiah decided to return to the plantation to see what was going on. Upon arrival, the exiles found the Federal army in charge and learned of the hasty retreat of his owner. However, they were all treated as "contraband", liberated property, and told they would receive food and shelter in exchange for work on the trenches or unloading ammunition wagons. Isaiah and family began to doubt the veracity and altruism of the blue-coated hordes, and realized they would not be treated any better by the victors than they were before. With some liberated livestock and other needful things in hand, the family retraced their steps back to the rock shelter, fed up with their prospects on the Edge plantation.

This story reflects the timeline when Stoneman left for the Moore's Bridge raid and Gen. Blair's infantry was called upon to fill in for the cavalry. To mask the raid, the infantry was to cause a diversion as if they were attempting to capture the Sandtown crossing. Large cannons were brought up and a duel began lasting more than a day. Confederates lobbed Reade shells and explosive polyhedral 3 1/2 and 4 1/2 inch balls to within yards of the Edge house.

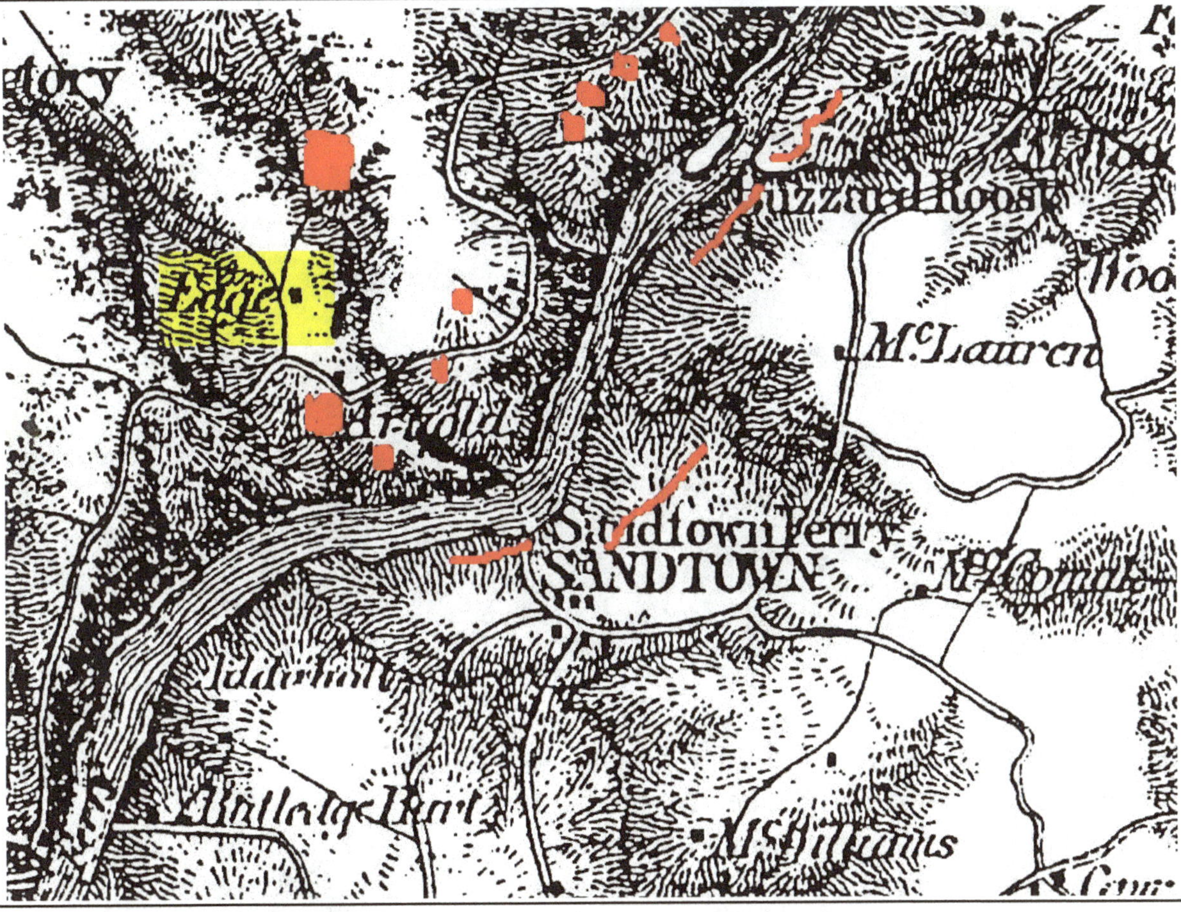

Detail of Sandtown, showing Federal and Confederate positions and the Edge house.

Remains of the Rock House on the road to the Sandtown Ferry.

Reade shell and fuse from the Edge property on the river at the Sandtown Ferry. The ground there was littered with shell fragments, fired Confederate and dropped Federal bullets of all kinds. Knapsack buckles, shirt and coat buttons as well as spurs and saddle parts were also found there (courtesy of Sweet Water Creek State Park).

Federal and Confederate Bullets from the Edge property: .44 and .50 balls CSA; Spencer cartridge Fed; Gardner CSA; Burnside, Starr carbine and .58 Williams .58 Enfield, Sharp's, Smith carbine and .58 Minne Fed.

One rule of thumb for Cavalry raids in this campaign, was that a raid by one side begets a counter-raid. No sooner had Stoneman left for Moore's Bridge, a party of Confederates, having crossed over Baker's Ferry, was reporting him gone. As soon as Stoneman returned from his raid, he reported a large force of enemy crossing the river at Aderholt's Ferry. This caused a great movement among the Federals, sure that they would be attacked by Confederate Cavalry. On July 20th, Gen. George Thomas reported that Stoneman's report "***...turns out to be a humbug... .***"

The army's great fear: a cavalry raid resulting in disrupted rail traffic and supply lines.

Meanwhile, information was coming into Sherman's possession that the failed Moore's bridge raid had caused a real panic in the Confederate command. A captured negro, attached to a Confederate Colonel, according to Stoneman, "*.. says our operations in the direction of Campbellton and Moore's Bridge caused the greatest stampede...(7-20-64).*"

Sherman now had three points where his men had crossed the river and were threatening Atlanta. Three great battles ensued: The Battle Of Atlanta, cutting the railroad to points east; The Battle of Peachtree Creek and The Battle of Ezra Church, west of Atlanta. Though the federals won all three engagements, they were no closer to final victory. Sherman knew he had to cut the railroads south and west of Atlanta.

Because the raid had caused so much consternation in the Confederate command, Sherman began planning a larger raid. On July 26th, he confided to Gen. Thomas that he had plans for McCook:

...I have consented to his dropping down the west bank of the Chattahoochee to a point about Campbellton, crossing there and striking out for the railroad ...

Sherman also ordered 5000 of Stoneman's Cavalry to go around Atlanta on the right, to meet up with McCook, about Lovejoy's Station, and fight their way back to their lines. Stoneman was also given the option of striking out for Macon, in a long shot attempt to free the Federal prisoners at Andersonville. All of this was not so secret, Confederate Gen. Ross reporting as early as the 24th, that pontoon boats were seen near Baker's Ferry: "*...There can be no doubt, I think, of this being a pontoon train, and the enemy in all probability intend crossing with a formidable force to strike the road below Atlanta...*"

Rails, atop piles of burning ties cause iron to soften so they can be twisted out of shape.

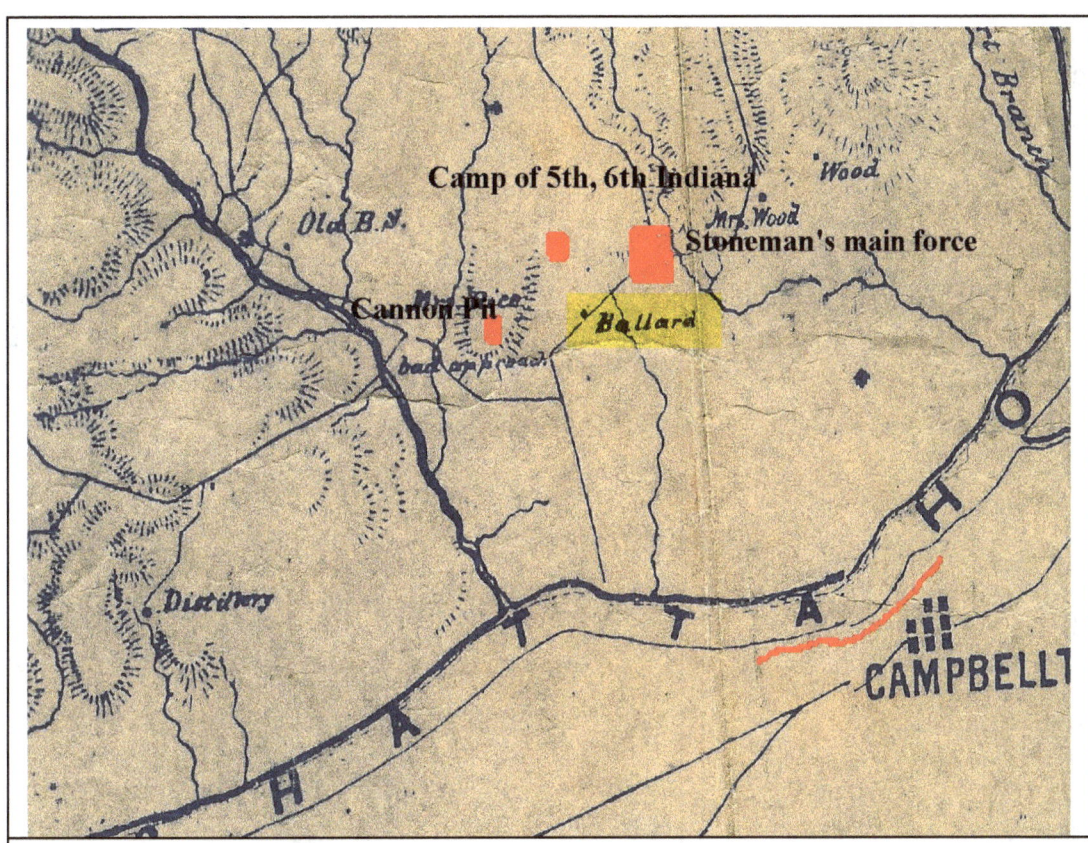
Capt. Merrill's map of Campbellton, showing Confederate and Federal positions.

On the 27th, McCook arrived at Campbellton and waited for the pontoon train of the Army of the Cumberland. He waited and waited until the element of surprise was completely dashed. He sent troopers with horses to help the underpowered pontoon train and moved down river to find another crossing. He found a ferry crossing, about six miles below, where today's West Chapel Hill road leads to the river. The road north leads into the Campbellton-Dallas Road, while the dirt road on the left leads to Smith's Ferry, which was operated by Moses Smith in 1864. His house on a hill overlooking the river was built in 1854 of sculptured brick. The many rooms are warmed by four brick chimneys and the front sports a Greek Revival columned front entrance.

By 1850, Moses Smith, his wife, two sons and two daughters enjoyed idyllic plantation life on the river. The plantation included 200 acres valued at $ 6000. There were 5 horses, 9 mules, 20 milk cows, 6 oxen and 30 beef cattle on land that produced 40 bushels of wheat, 750 of Indian corn, 100 of sweet potatoes and 100 pounds of butter a year.

McCook's Raid:
1st Brigade: Col. John Croxton
  8th Iowa
  4th Kentucky
  1st Tennessee
2nd Brigade: Lt. Col. William. H. Torrey
  2nd Indiana
  4th Indiana
  1st Wisconsin

Artillery: 1 section 18th Indiana Battery

Harrison's Brigade: Col. Thomas J. Harrison
  2nd Kentucky
  8th Indiana
  5th Iowa
  9th Ohio
  4th Tennessee

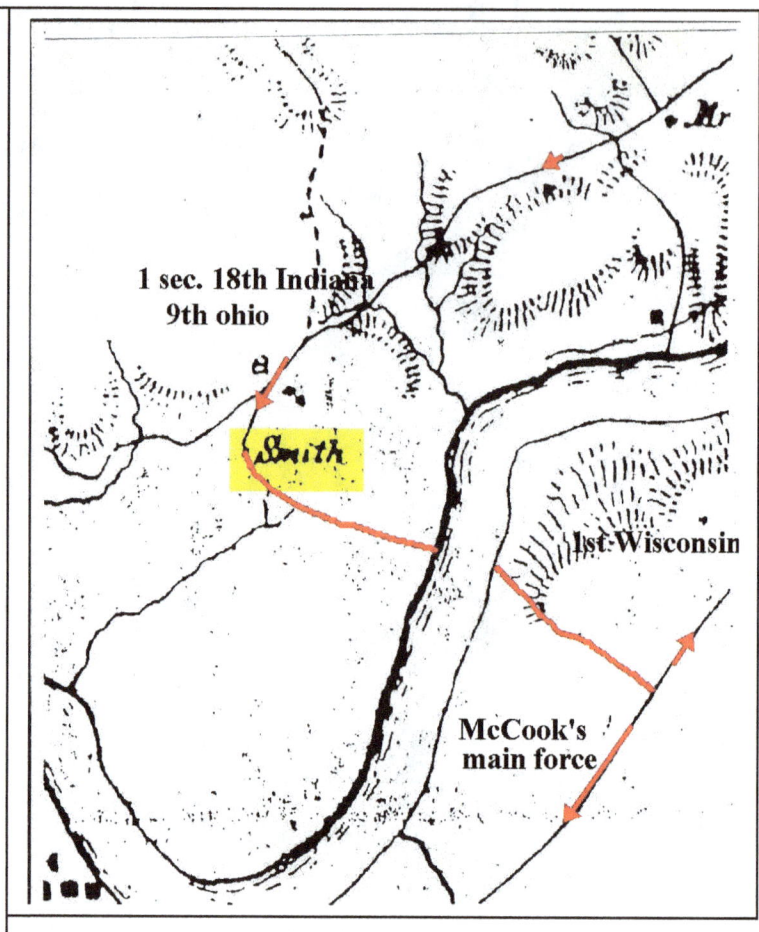

Capt. Merrill's map of Smith's Ferry, with annotation.

3500 MEN WITH HORSES, LOOKING FOR THE FERRY OPERATOR:

The ferry was found after McCook realized he would be unable to cross at Campbellton. His long stay there on the 28th, due to the slow progress of the pontoon train, had alerted the Confederate defenders in town. Moving south on present day Highway 166, McCook found a spot near the home of Moses M. Smith and prepared to cross. Once again the progress of the pontoon train proved an ill omen to the whole affair.

Judge Byron Mathews later wrote in **The McCook-Stoneman Raid**:

...By sunrise, he was at Smith's Ferry, six miles to the south. At this point the approaches were good and he could move without difficulty ...A Confederate scout, captured in the search, reported the east bank undefended, and not wishing to lose more time, McCook decided to move ahead. Croxton's men (4th

Kentucky mounted, 8th Iowa and lst Tennessee) found a single bateau on the river bank. It was pressed into service and paddled back and forth across the river for over six hours, carrying four men at a time. By noon, when the pontoon train arrived, his brigade was on the east bank and secure in position.

After the crossing, the 9th Ohio Cavalry, commanded by William D. Hamilton, and one section of the l8th Indiana Battery, commanded by Lt. William Rippetoe, were detached and ordered to protect the pontoon train.

The lst Wisconsin Cavalry, under the command of Major Nathan Paine, was also detached and ordered to check the road to Campbellton and, if possible, to rejoin the column at or near Fayetteville...

While waiting for the pontoon train, he ordered four men at a time to cross on a small bateau, leading their horses. After several hours, Maj. Paine's lst Wisconsin was across and heading back toward Campbellton. After the train arrived and all were across, McCook set out to destroy the railroad.

Once across the river, McCook's men headed for Palmetto station. Meeting no opposition, they destroyed the depot, the track and wagon train. Between Fairburn and Lovejoy's station another 300 wagons and 600 mules were destroyed. They were to meet General Stoneman's force from the east at Lovejoy's and combine their efforts in destroying the Macon railroad. Stoneman, however, was nowhere to be found. He had, in fact, followed his wild dream of reaching beyond Macon and freeing the prisoners at Andersonville. The disposition of McCook and his men were secondary in consideration.

Amid this confusion, the Confederate cavalry arrived on the scene. Arrnstrong's and Ferguson's horsemen began pushing the raiders back toward Newnan. The next day, the Confederate Infantry arrived on the scene by train. There was a rout in the making.

Stoneman's fate was no better as he was being pursued by Confederates at Macon. A few days later, near Clinton, Ga. Stoneman and 500 remaining troopers surrendered to Confederate General Iverson. All this left McCook holding the bag: he began a retreat back toward Newnan and had several encounters with superior enemy forces. At Brown's Mill he lost his Artillery, most of his equipment and about 500 men. The remainder fled to Wedowee, Alabama, recrossed the river and returned to Marietta via Buchanan and Draketown, Ga.

Federal troops removing rails from an Atlanta railroad, ties stacked in the background used to heat rails for twisting

FIRST HAND ACCOUNTS OF THE MCCOOK RAID:

James W. Godwin, 4th Tennessee Cavalry, from his personal diary:

July 26th (SIC). Crossed the river and took the Sandtown road, and passed through Palmetto, Ga., about 9 o'clock in the night. Here we burned about 5,000 bales of cotton belonging to the Confederacy about 3 o'clock in the morning. Going south we captured Gen. Hood's wagon train; orders to burn the wagons and contents. After firing some of the wagons loaded with old guns and the guns being loaded, we concluded to chop the others down as it was not healthy to be close around when the old muskets commenced discharging their contents. The convalescent men and horses of the different companies of the regiment, 4th Tennessee Cavalry, with the pack train of mules, were left and went into camps.

July 28th (sic). All quite in our camps today; hear some heavy cannonading in front once and awhile during the day. The command started to destroy the railroad at or near Macon, then proceed east and join Gen. Stoneman in the rear of Atlanta. These two forces united could have held their own with any force the Confederacy could have sent against them. The command remained at Macon too long after doing the work they went to do, the rebs run cavalry, infantry and artillery against them and had the command nearly surrounded. At Newman Gen. McCook would have surrendered the whole command if it had not been for that gallant and brave lieutenant-colonel, James Brownlow, of the 1st Tenn. Cavalry. He fought his way out and saved most of the command.

It was here that Gen. McCook held a council with the commanders of the brigades and regiments and was preparing to surrender when Brownlow came rushing out and said they could not surrender the First Tennessee Cavalry. Our Senior Major Meshack Stephens, who was here in command of the 4th Tennessee Cavalry, said nor could they surrender the 4th Tennessee Cavalry and told Brownlow he would go out with him. This was an inspiration for the other regiments and most of them followed the First and Fourth Tennessee Cavalry out, which was done by cutting way through the rebel lines which were all around our forces. Gen. McCook and headquarters took courage and went out with those who fought out. So close was the fight that our men in cutting through one place, the rebs after emptying their guns, the enemy being on our retreating ranks and then pitched rails endwise into our ranks. Many of the men were wounded. H. Stephens of Co. I, was badly shot in the back or hips, but was taken out. A.J. Hickman of Co. E was killed on the field. J.S. Roberts of same company, was wounded and brought out.

The Capture of Logan Howell, 5th Iowa Cavalry:

"The next expedition in which the regiment participated began with the accomplishment of the most brilliant results, and ended most disastrously. On July 23rd, the Fifth Iowa Cavalry, with the other troops composing the command of Colonel Harrison, marched to the relief of General Stoneman, whose force had been picketing the Chattahoochee River from Sweet Water to Nick-a-Jack Creek. The command marched all night, arriving at the river at noon the next day. The enemy was posted on the opposite side of the river. The Fifth Iowa Cavalry was ordered to report to General McCook. The regiment marched up the river six miles, crossed on a pontoon bridge, and reported at General McCook's headquarters, when it was ordered to proceed to Vining's Station and draw three days' rations, and then rejoin the command. The rations were drawn, the regiment

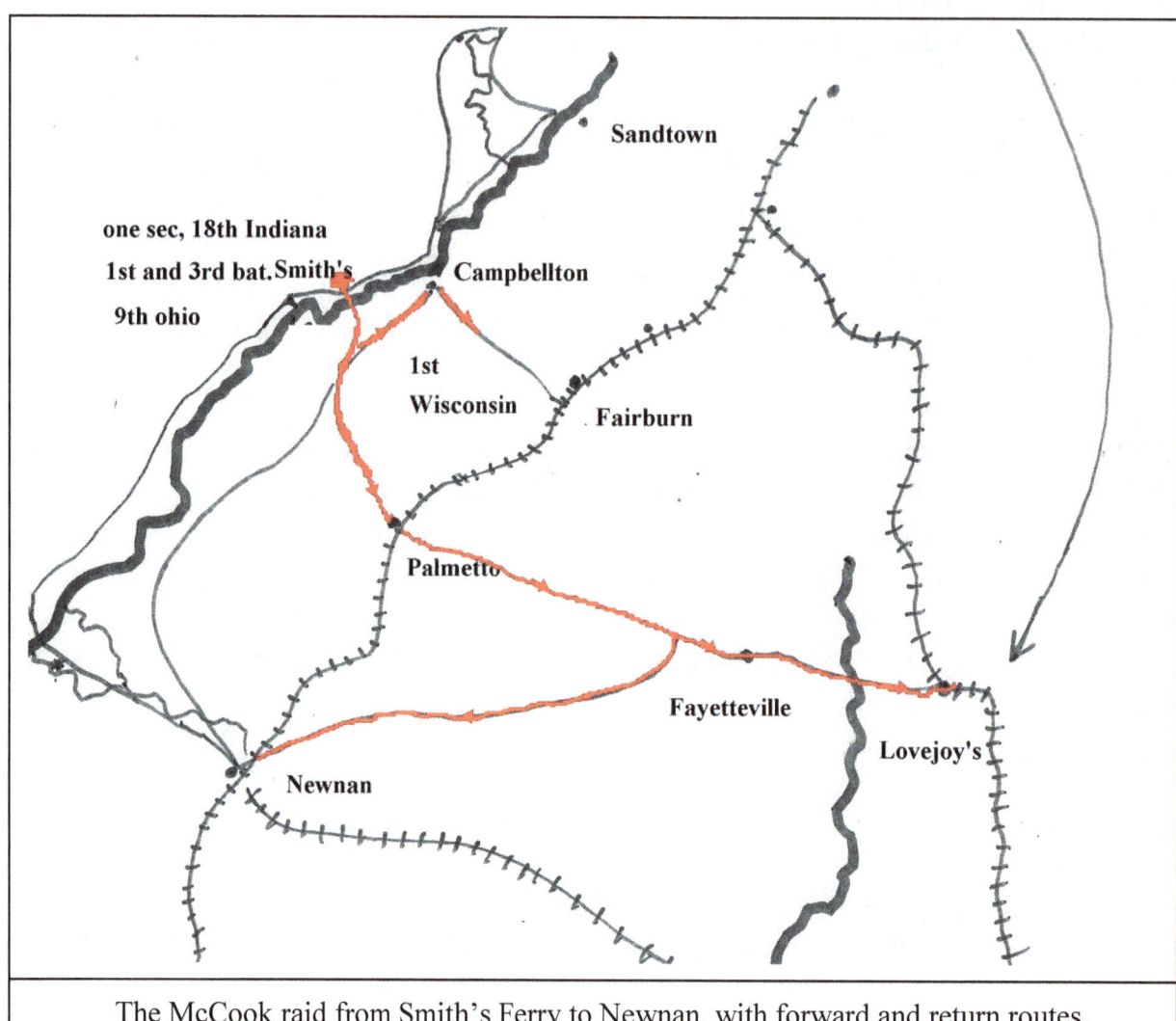

The McCook raid from Smith's Ferry to Newnan, with forward and return routes.

joined the command of General McCook and, at noon of July 26th, started with that command on the memorable raid to the rear of Atlanta. The object of the raid was the destruction of the enemy's communications on the Atlanta and Macon Railroad, the objective point being Lovejoy's Station. All the afternoon and the following night the march was continued down the Chattahoochee River, and, at sunrise on July 28th, the command had reached a point opposite Campbellton, where a force of the enemy was posted. The troops marched on down the river to a point five miles below Campbellton, where a pontoon bridge was laid across the river, upon which the troops crossed and pushed rapidly forward, reaching Palmetto Station, on the Atlanta and West Point Railroad, about dark. Here about 600 of the enemy were stationed, who, after a slight skirmish were driven off, and the depot fired, the telegraph wire torn down, and the railroad track torn up for a short distance. After completing the work of destruction the troops moved on, the

Fifth Iowa Cavalry acting as rear guard, and the march continuing until a train of 500 wagons, containing the extra baggage of the rebel army at Atlanta, was overtaken and captured, together with the 250 officers and men who were guarding it, and 2,000 fine mules and horses, the troops pushed forward to Lovejoy's station, the objective point of the expedition, and, upon arriving there, destroyed a portion of the track of the Atlanta and Macon Railroad, and burned the depot.

"The results of the expedition had thus far been eminently successful and the damage inflicted upon the enemy very great. The commanding General of the rebel cavalry now concentrated his forces rapidly for the purpose of intercepting and cutting off the retreat of the Union troops engaged in this daring raid, and the return march was replete with disaster to General McCook's command. After leaving Lovejoy's Station the troops marched rapidly, with the Fifth Iowa Cavalry in advance and the Eighth Iowa Cavalry as rear guard. The troops had marched but a few miles, however, when the rear guard was fiercely attacked, and the Eighth Iowa lost two officers and seven men killed, and fourteen men wounded in the fight which ensued. Part of the command turned back to assist the Eighth Iowa, and the enemy was repulsed. In the meantime, the Fifth Iowa, marching rapidly in advance, came to the bridge over Flint River, and found the enemy in the act of firing it. After a brisk encounter the enemy was driven off, and the regiment crossed the bridge, accompanied by the artillery---two Parrott guns, which were quickly placed in position to cover the bridge, the Fifth Iowa taking position in support of the guns. In a short time the rest of General McCook's command arrived, closely pursued by the enemy, but succeeded in crossing the bridge, which was then destroyed. The Fifth Iowa Cavalry again took the advance on the road leading to Fayetteville, but, after marching for two miles, was ordered back to the main command, which had not moved. Again the regiment was ordered to advance on the same road, and again ordered to return after going about the same distance. Three precious hours were lost by this vacillation and delay. Finally, at dark, General McCook sent four companies of the Fifth Iowa to the rear, with orders to remain and report the movements of the enemy. The balance of the regiment was placed in front, with Company H, commanded by Lieutenant Hays, in the advance, with orders to charge, if he encountered the enemy, and keep the road clear for the advance of the rest of the command. Soon after the march was resumed, the advance encountered a force of the enemy. A charge was promptly made and the rebels were repulsed and driven away, without scarcely interrupting the march of the main column. The march was continued during the night, but slow progress was made on account of the difficulty of keeping the prisoners and a large number of captured horses and mules well under guard. At 10 A.M., July 30th, the advance reached the town of Newnan, where a force of ,000 (sic) rebels had taken position. Major Beard, with five companies of the Fifth Iowa and two companies of the Eighth Indiana, charged into the town, but was unable to dislodge the enemy. General McCook then ordered the Fifth Iowa and Eighth Indiana to remain in line of battle and hold the enemy in check, while he moved the rest of the command, and the prisoners, around the town to the left. The movement occupied two hours, and compelled the command to march at least five miles out of a direct course, thereby enabling the enemy to concentrate a large force to resist the further advance of the column. About four miles from Newnan, this force was encountered. The two Parrott guns were placed in position and shelled the enemy vigorously. The enemy made three separate charges upon the guns, fighting desperately for their possession, but each charge was repulsed, and the guns continued their fire until the ammunition was exhausted. The guns were then spiked, the wheels cut down and, thus rendered useless, they were abandoned. General McCook found his command completely surrounded by a greatly superior force under the command of the rebel General Wheeler. The situation was most desperate. Orders were given to each regiment to charge and cut its way through the enemy's lines. After desperate fighting and heavy loss, all the regiments, except the Eighth Iowa, succeeded in cutting their way through the rebel forces. The Eighth Iowa, being ordered to cover the rear, was cut off by the enemy and nearly all captured. The regiments which succeeded in getting through the lines of the enemy did not all get together again, but reached the Chattahoochee River at different places. General McCook, with the Fifth Iowa, Eighth Indiana, and Fourth Tennessee Cavalry, arrived at Philpot Ferry about midnight, and commenced crossing the troops on the ferry boat. The Eighth Indiana had succeeded in getting across when the enemy appeared in force and attacked the remainder of the command. Finding themselves opposed to overwhelming numbers, most of the men abandoned their horses, and a considerable number of them escaped by swimming the river. The mounted men, under General McCook, continued to retreat, and reached Marietta five days later. The dismounted men took to the woods in small parties and many were captured, while some escaped and reached the Union lines at different points, after suffering great hardships from hunger and exposure. They were constantly pursued, and it was marvelous that any of them succeeded in avoiding capture. The loss of the Fifth Iowa Cavalry in this raid was heavy. First Lieutenant Andrew Guler, of Company E was killed; First Lieutenant William T. Hays, of Company H, was taken prisoner, and 119 enlisted men were killed, wounded and captured." (Howell was captured on July 31st and spent the remainder of the war in Andersonville prison.)

--- From *Historical Sketch, Fifth Regiment Iowa Volunteer Cavalry*, Roster and Record of Iowa Soldiers During the War of Rebellion Volume IV, 1910

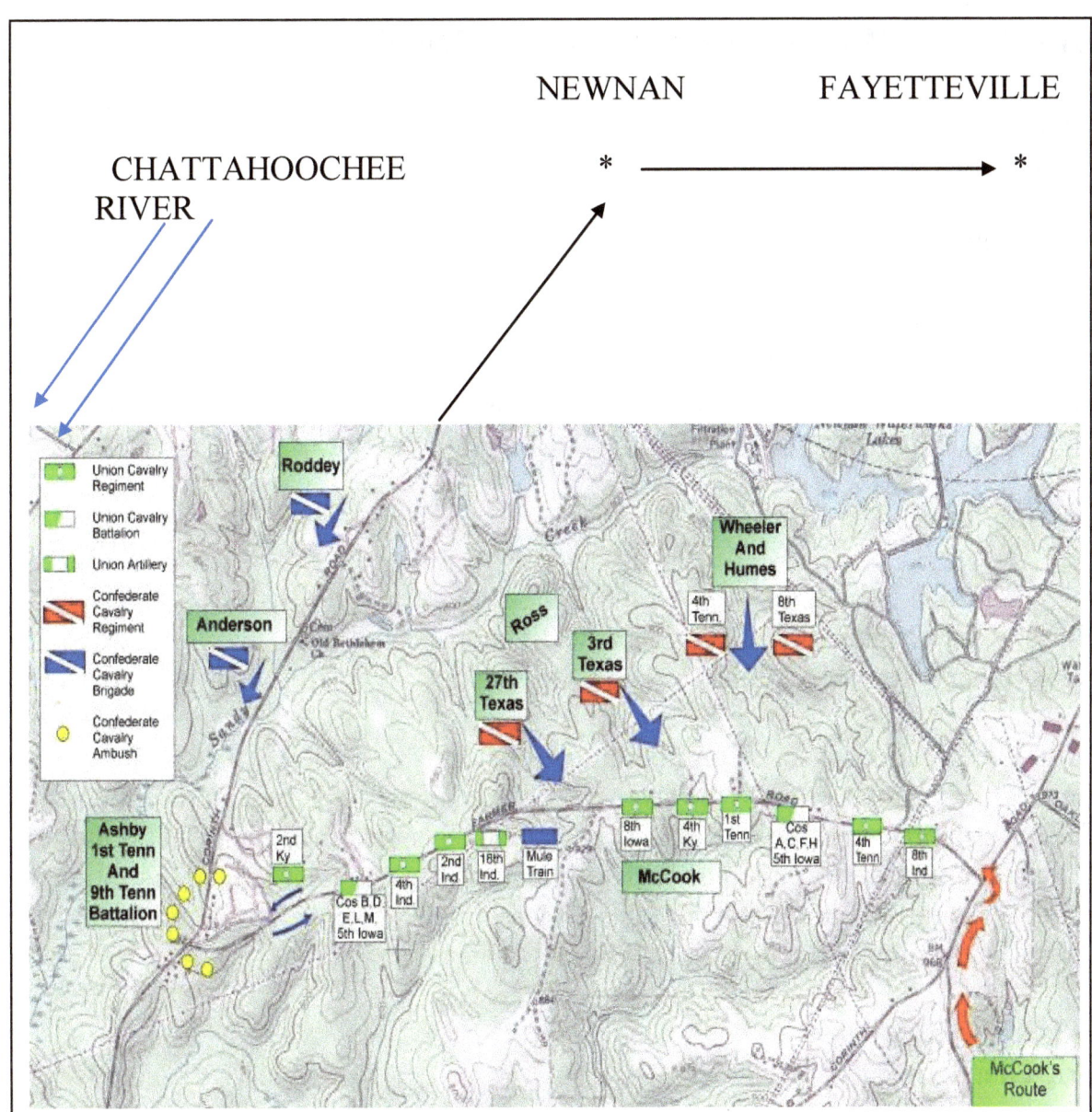

The Battle of Browns Mill, south of Newnan. McCook and others barely escaped, crossing the Chattahoochee below Moore's burned bridge making their way to Marietta.

OFFICIAL REPORTS JULY 15 - AUGUST 3

CSA
Atlanta, July 15, 1864

His excellency Jefferson Davis,
Richmond, Va.:
The enemy were driven back across the Chattahoochee near Newnan this morning by our cavalry before they reached the West Point Railroad. Another corps of infantry has crossed above (Atlanta). Nearly all available stores and machinery are removed, and the people have mostly evacuated the town.

Braxton Bragg.

Hqtrs. Ross' Brigade, Jackson's Cavalry Division,
Near Baker's Ferry, Ga., July 16, 1864 - 8:10 p.m.

Brig.-Gen. W.H. Jackson, Commanding Division:
General: My scouts crossed the river near Baker's Ferry this p.m. and found no Federal infantry this side of Ruff's Station. Citizen's informed them that it moved off last night in the direction of Roswell Factory. One cavalry brigade is camped about three miles from Baker's Ferry. Two regiments of cavalry passed down the river this evening in the direction of Sweet Water.

L.S. Ross,
Brigadier-Gen.

Richmond, July 17, 1864

General J. E. Johnston:
Lt.-Gen. J.B. Hood has been commissioned to the temporary rank of General under the state law of Congress. I am directed by the Sec. of War to inform you that as you have failed to arrest the advance of the enemy to the vicinity of Atlanta, far in the interior of Georgia, and express no confidence that you can defeat or repel him, you are hereby relieved of the command of the Army and the Dept. of Tennessee, which you will immediately turn over to General Hood.

S. Cooper, Adjutant and Inspector-General.

FED
Hqtrs. Cavalry Command,
July 18, 1864 -10 p.m.

Major-Gen. George H. Thomas:
General: Col. Adams, commanding brigade guarding the river near the mouth of Sweet Water, has just reported to me that the enemy are crossing the river in force above the mouth of the creek, with what object or intent has not yet transpired.

George Stoneman,
Major-Gen.

Hqtrs. Military Division of the Mississippi,
In the field, July 19, 1864.

Gen. Thomas:
...What about the report of Stoneman about the enemy crossing the Chattahoochee westward at Sweet Water? I think it was a party sent to prevent Stoneman's return from West Point, whither they supposed he had gone...

W.T. Sherman,
Major-Gen.

Hqtrs. Army of the Ohio,
In the field, Ga., July19, 1864.

Col. E.W. Crittendon,
Commanding Cavalry Brigade, Isham's Ferry, Ga.:
Col.: Gen. Stoneman reports that the enemy is crossing the river at the mouth of Sweet Water. They will doubtless attempt to destroy our trains and depot at Marietta, and may attempt to capture our bridges at the different river crossings. Keep all trains on this side of the river and under your guns. Look out for the rebels and give them a warm reception. Keep me informed of all that you learn. The supply train is ordered forward tonight.

Another target of cavalry raids. Federal troops putting up telegrah poles and wire.

J.M. Schofield,
Major-Gen., Commanding

Hqtrs. Cavalry Command,
July 19, 1864.

Major-Gen. George H. Thomas:
General: The force that crossed the river last night is supposed to be a strong scouting party.

Geo. Stoneman
Major-Gen.

Hqtrs. Cavalry Command, Dept. of the Ohio,
July 19, 1864 - 11 a.m.

Major-Gen. Thomas, Commanding, &c.:

I have ascertained that the rebel party that crossed the river last night near the mouth of Sweet Water Creek, probably recrossed this morning, as I cannot hear of their having gone northward, nor that they brought over any horses. The enemy's pickets near Turner's Ferry and the mouth of Nickajack were very active and unusually spiteful all night and this morning, and I have strengthened the line, keeping a limited reserve at the most central position. He appears strongest near the mouth of Sweet Water, a large cavalry camp being there.

I learned that several parties of several hundred in each party made their appearance in the country we passed over, crossing at Campbellton after we left there, three days ago. The enemy have facilities for crossing, as he has all the boats on their side, which are sunk when not required. I have one brigade near the mouth of Sweet Water watching the force opposite, another near the mouth of Nickajack, the dismounted men at Turner's Ferry, all connecting. My remaining force, acting as reserve, and to guard our communications, is at and near the Widow Mitchell's, and from this I also send out scouts beyond the Sweet Water Town Bridge. I will keep you, and through you, the commanding general, informed of everything of importance as it transpires.

(Forwarded to Gen. Sherman by Gen. Thomas)
George Stoneman, Major-Gen., Commanding.

Hqtrs. Army of the Cumberland,
July 20, 1864 - 12 m.

Major-Gen. W.T. Sherman,
Commanding Military Division of the Mississippi:
General: ....P.S. - The Stoneman raid turns out to be a humbug. I sent you his last report yesterday afternoon and hope it was received. It seems that when twenty-five of the enemy are seen anywhere, they are considered in force.

Geo. H. Thomas,
Major-Gen., U.S. Volunteers, Commanding.

July 20, 1864 - 11a.m.

Major-Gen. Sherman, Commanding, &c.:

A negro, who was taken prisoner with Col. Streight, has just come in, and, I think, brings reliable information, and, if reliable, is very important, to wit, that Johnston is retreating in haste, along the Macon Road. A captain, who deserted, and comes to us, says that Johnston cannot go by the way of West Point, as the gauge is different the other side of the river from this side. The negro says our operations in the direction of Campbellton and Moore's Bridge caused the greatest stampede; that Jackson's Division has gone to the Blue Mountain in Alabama; that he saw Wheeler near Campbellton, and that his whole force near there and below; that there is no force in Atlanta but the "new issue" (militia); that the army is utterly demoralized and easily frightened...

George Stoneman,
Major-Gen.

Hqtrs. Military Division of the Mississippi,
In the field, July 20, 1864 - 8p.m.

Gen. Thomas: Dear General: I have just read Gen. Stoneman's letter, with your endorsement. We have seen enough today to convince us that all of Stoneman's information is incorrect. Something more than militia remain at Atlanta, and they are not demoralized... If we cannot break in, we must move by the right flank and interpose between the river and Atlanta, and operate against the road south...

W.T. Sherman,
Major-Gen.

CSA
Hqtrs. Ross' Brigade, Jackson's Cavalry Division,
McGhee's, Ga., July 24, 1864 - 8a.m.

Brigadier-Gen. Jackson,
Commanding Division:
General: A large train of wagons can be seen from the hills near Baker's Ferry on opposite side of the river, between that point and Green's, and a woman has just come to my headquarters from that side of the river. She says she left the Baker's Ferry Road, about a half a mile from Ferry, yesterday evening, walking several miles down the river, where she crossed. She saw Col. Adams' brigade cavalry and some infantry, but could not tell the number. The infantry had stopped and stacked

arms on the Baker's Ferry Road. She saw two of my men taken before Col. Adams, and saw the boats in which the party crossed the river yesterday below Baker's (only two of Capt. Northsworthy's men were captured), and said the boats looked like cloth. They placed the boats in wagons on their return, and she saw many others in wagons along with this force. My scouts confirm the statement in reference to the brigade of cavalry, wagon train, &c., but have not discovered infantry. There can be no doubt, I think, of this being a pontoon train, and the enemy, in all probability intend crossing with a formidable force to strike the road below Atlanta. I have strengthened my pickets on that line. I believe the statement of the woman about the infantry...

L.S. Ross'
Brigadier-Gen.

Pontoon boats on wagons.

FED
July 26, 1864.

Major-Gen. Sherman,
Commanding, &c.:

In case we succeed in carrying out your wishes will it meet your approbation, should I see a good opening, if I should with a portion of the command make a dash on Macon and by a vigorous stroke release the prisoners (officers) now at that point, and afterward go on to Americus and release those (privates) there. I would like to try it, and am willing to run any risks, and I can vouch for my little command. Now is the time to do it before the rebel army falls back and covers that country, and I have every inducement to try it. If we accomplish the desired object it will compensate for the loss as prisoners of us all, and I shall feel compensated for almost any sacrifice,

George Stoneman,
Major-Gen.

Near Atlanta, Ga., July 26, 1864 - 9p.m.

(Received. 1p.m. 27th.)

Maj.-General Halleck,
Washington, D.C.:
Tomorrow we begin the move against Atlanta...At the same time I send by the right a force of about 3,500 cavalry, under Gen. McCook, and round by the left, about 5,000 cavalry, under Stoneman, with orders to reach the railroad about Griffin. I have also consented that Stoneman (after he has executed this part of the plan), if he finds it feasible, may, with his division proper (about 2,000) go to Macon and attempt the release of our officers, prisoners there, and then to Anderson (ville) to release the 20,000 of our men, prisoners there. This is probably more than he can accomplish, but it is worthy of a determined effort. While these are in progress I will, with the main army give employment to all of the rebel army still in Atlanta.

W.T. Sherman,
Major-Gen.

Hqtrs. Military Division of the Mississippi,
In the field, near Atlanta, Ga., July 26, 1864.

Gen. Thomas:
Gen. McCook represents the enemy cavalry to his front entrenched behind good works, extending from about White Hall down to the Chattahoochee, and he apprehended difficulty in breaking through. I have consented to his dropping down the west bank of the Chattahoochee to a point about Campbellton, crossing there and striking out for the railroad. This will turn the position of the cavalry, and force them back to meet General McCook on more open ground.

W.T. Sherman.
Major-Gen., Commanding.

Hqtrs. First Cav. Div., Dept. of the Cumberland.
Opposite Campbellton, July 27, 1864 - 9p.m.

Capt. L.M. Dayton,
Aide-de-Camp:

I arrived opposite Campbellton at 4 p.m. The rebels have the whole river picketed in this vicinity, though not in sufficient force to have prevented my crossing. The pontoon train, however, at the hour I write, is not yet within six miles of me. Capt. Kossak found it impossible to pull it with his mules. I will take some of my cavalry horses and pull it up. This delay will involve the probable necessity of crossing below here, as the attention of the enemy has, I think, been attracted to this point for some reason, as there have been none of them here recently until last night, when a brigade came down to picket their different ferries. I have endeavored to conceal my force, and think the rebels are not yet seriously alarmed. I expected to have reached Fayetteville tonight, and but for the disability on the part of the pontoon train would have done so.

I now think that I will be able to cross by daybreak at some point. Nothing has been found on this side of the river except small scouting parties of Texas cavalry. It is twenty-six miles from here to the point from which we moved our camp this morning.

E.M. McCook,
Brigadier-Gen.,
Commanding Division.

9th Ohio Cavalry Guidon.

CSA
Confidential.
Hqtrs., &c., July 26, 1864 - 10 a.m.

Major-Gen. Wheeler,
Commanding, &c.:
Gen. Hood directs that you put Kelly's division in motion toward Campbellton alone, and that you and Gen. Kelly report in person at these headquarters without delay.

F.A. Shoup.
Chief of Staff.

Atlanta, July 28, 1864 - 6:20 p.m.

Gov. Joseph E. Brown,
Macon, Ga.:

Raid on our right checked at Flat Rock. Enemy reported as crossing at Campbellton and at Varner's for raid. Cavalry sent to meet it. Send troops to Griffin.

J.B. Hood, General.

Hqtrs. Army of Tennessee,
July 29, 1864 - 4:30 a.m.

Gen. Joseph Wheeler, Commanding Cavalry:
Your dispatch of yesterday, 6:30 p.m., just received. At same time one from Gen. Jackson, dated near Campbellton, 28th, 9 p.m., stating that the force which crossed the river near that point was McCook's cavalry division. They were evidently making for the Macon and Western Railroad, moving via Fairburn. The commanding Gen. directs that you send a force to co-operate with Gen. Jackson, moving across to such point as you may deem best calculated to intercept the enemy. Use your own discretion in selecting force, and in general instructions given them. It is intended that you should exercise your own judgement in detaching this force from your command. Gen. Jackson says:

I move in an hour to Fairburn, thence below to intercept or strike them in flank, and shall endeavor to protect railroad.

He has two brigades - Harrison's and Ross' - and will probably require assistance.

L.P. Dodge, Aide-de-Camp
(for Brigadier-Gen. Shoup.)

Hqtrs. Army of Tennessee,
July 29, 1864 - 2 p.m.

Gen. Wheeler:
A raid from the left has struck the Macon Railroad below Jonesborough about six miles. Troops have gone from here by rail. Important to prevent damage as far as possible. There is armed militia below on the road; should be advanced to prevent destruction north. Take such steps as your judgement suggests. Force unknown.

F.A. Shoup,
Chief of Staff.

P.S. - Have not heard from Jackson this evening.

July 29, 1864 - 3:45 p.m.

Major-Gen. Wheeler, Commanding: ...Gen. Hood desires your return very much as soon as you can get through with those fellows in rear. He has important service for you.

F.A. Shoup,
Chief of Staff.

Hqtrs. Army of Tennessee,
July 29, 1864 - 6:20 p.m.

Gen. Wheeler, Commanding cavalry:
Your dispatch of 1:15 p.m. just received. Jackson engaged the raid from the west at 3 p.m. Enemy said to be 3,000 strong. Infantry sent; 3,000 militia at Macon; some directed to be sent to Griffin. Send information south when important to them.

F.A. Shoup,
Chief of Staff.

8th Texas Cavalry flag.

Two miles and a half from Fayetteville,
July 29, 1864 - 10 p.m.

Gen. Wheeler,
Commanding Cavalry Corps:
General: The latest reports represent the enemy moving toward Fayetteville. I am quite certain they are moving back to cross the Chattahoochee. I have Harrison's brigade in their front at Fayetteville, and am moving now with Ross' brigade to that place. Should enemy attempt to pass round the place I will gain their front or flank about Newnan. If you can follow and push them in rear it would be well.

W.H. Jackson,
Brigadier-Gen.

July 29, 1864 - 6:45 p.m.

Gen. Armstrong, Commanding, &c.:
Gen. Hood desires you to keep your scouts active about the Etowah. Send some of them across the river. He wants to know what is going on about Sweet Water and in that region.

F.A. Shoup,
Chief of Staff.

5TH Georgia Cavalry flag.

Atlanta, July 29, 1864 - 5:45 p.m.

Gen. W.H. Jackson,
Commanding cavalry between Jonesborough and Lovejoy's:
An infantry brigade (700) went down by rail several hours ago. Hume's cavalry also ordered against your raiders should you need more force.

J.B. Hood, General.

FED
Hqtrs. Military Division of the Mississippi,
In the field near Atlanta, Ga., July 30, 1864.

Gen. Thomas:
Send two or three of your best scouts across to the west bank of the Chattahoochee, and down till they come to where Gen. McCook crossed with his pontoons. Ascertain if the bridge is still down and guarded, and with orders to send us back word and news from our cavalry.

W.T. Sherman,
Major-Gen., Commanding.

Gen. Roddy, 4th Alabama Cav. arrived at Newnan and fought McCook at Brownsville.

Hqtrs. Military Division of the Mississippi,

In the field, near Atlanta, Ga., July 31, 1864.

Gen. Thomas:
I have further news of McCook. The officer who commands the pontoon train is back with his boats at Vining's. At 2 p.m. on Friday Gen. McCook was across at Rivertown with 3,000 men and started out. That night the officer saw large fires in the direction of the railroad. He was ordered to come back to Vining's with his boat train by Gen. McCook, who expected to come back by a circuit north.

W.T. Sherman,
Major-Gen., Commanding.

Hqtrs. Military Division of the Mississippi,
In the field, near Atlanta, Ga., July 31, 1864.

Gen. Thomas:
...I think I appreciate Gen. Garrard's good qualities, but he is so cautious that if forced to make a bold move to the relief of Gen. McCook I doubt if he would attempt it. Gen. Stoneman went with full knowledge of his risk; but Gen. McCook will have reason to expect co-operation from about McDonough, and may be disappointed when he finds his bridge gone and a new road ahead closed by Wheeler. He has, however, a bold and well-appointed force and can fight his way back; still for his sake, we must occupy the attention of the enemy as much as possible.

W.T. Sherman,
Major-Gen., Commanding.

Hqtrs. Military Division of the Mississippi,
In the field, near Atlanta, Ga., July 31, 1864.

Generals Thomas and Howard:
...I will send a regiment of cavalry down the west bank of the Chattahoochee to feel for Gen. McCook. I must have a bolder commander for Gen. Garrard's cavalry and want Gen. Thomas to name to me General Kilpatrick or some good brigadier for the command.

W.T. Sherman,

Major-Gen., Commanding.

Hqtrs. Army of the Ohio,
In the field, Ga., July 31, 1864.

Col. Israel Garrard,
Commanding Seventh Ohio Cavalry:
Col.: In compliance with orders from Major-Gen. Sherman, you will move with your regiment across the Chattahoochee at or near the Railroad Bridge; thence down the west bank of the river to a point (under-stood to be near Campbellton) where Gen. McCook left his pontoon bridge after crossing the river on his present raid. The object of your expedition is to aid Gen. McCook in recrossing the river on his return. It is understood that Gen. McCook left a regiment of cavalry with his bridge for the above purpose. If you find this to be the case, you will join that regiment and act in concert with it in carrying out Gen. McCook's instructions. In any event, you will watch carefully for Gen. McCook's troops for some distance up and down the river... You will use your utmost endeavors to assist Gen. McCook's troops in a safe passage of the river...

J.M. Schofield,
Major-Gen., Commanding.

CSA
July 31, 1864 - 4:15 p.m.

Lt. Gen. Hardee, Commanding Corps:
The following dispatch just received from Gen. Wheeler:

We fought the enemy from last night until tonight, killing and capturing many. We have thus far succeeded in keeping between them and the river, and they are showing evident signs of demoralization, having abandoned all their artillery, ambulance train, a large number of horses and mules, strewing the road with their arms and accouterments, and releasing 300 of our people, whom they captured with the wagon trains at Fayetteville.

F.A. Shoup,
Chief of Staff.

Atlanta, July 31, 1864 10:10 p.m.

Major-Gen. Maurey,
Montgomery, Ala.:
Can you send me some artillery and some small arm ammunition? I dispatch an officer to you on this business. We have killed, captured, or dispersed the raid that struck the Macon Road. Have their artillery, horses, &c.

J.B. Hood,
General.

The 1st Wisconsin Cavalry reunion 1880. Major Paine and 8 others were killed near Campbellton, in an ambush by Confederate Cavalry.

FED
Near Atlanta, Ga., August 1, 1864 - 8 p.m.
(Received 1:30 p.m. 2d.)

Maj.-Gen. Halleck,
Washington, D.C.:
Col. Brownlow reports from Marietta that he just reached there, having escaped from a disaster that overtook Gen. McCook's cavalry expedition at Newnan. He reports the expedition reached the railroad and destroyed more road than the rebels can repair in fifteen days, and burned 500 baggage wagons, including the headquarters trains of the rebel army, but was overtaken at Newnan by rebel cavalry and infantry, and after a hard fight had to surrender. Col. Harrison was killed. I can hardly believe it, as he had 3,000 picked cavalry... The loss of this cavalry is a serious one to me, but we are pushing the enemy close...

W.T. Sherman,
Major-Gen.

Hqtrs, Chief of Cavalry, Dept. of the Cumberland,
August 1, 1864.

Gen. Judson Kilpatrick, Cartersville, Ga.:
Proceed with your division to Chattahoochee River, taking the Sandtown Road. Should you find any stragglers from First Division, bring them up with you. ...

W.L. Elliott,
Brig.-Gen. and Chief of Cavalry.

Vining's, August 1, 1864 -9 a.m.

Major J.A. Campbell,
Asst. Adjutant-Gen. Dept. of the Ohio:
I have the honor to report that the Ninth Ohio Cavalry, the regiment left by Gen. McCook in charge of the pontoon train, returned here with it the day after he crossed, as ordered to do by Gen. McCook. The regiment has no orders with regard to watching the river for his return. The First Wisconsin Cavalry, part of Gen. McCook's command, came back the next morning after he crossed the river, and is now in camp somewhere in this vicinity. The Ninth Ohio Volunteer Cavalry and the First Wisconsin Cavalry are under the command of Col. Hamilton, Ninth Ohio Volunteer Cavalry. The ranking officer, Col. Hamilton, is not here at present: he left here an hour ago for headquarters of Gen. Sherman. Under these circumstances I have deemed it proper to report the facts and await your orders to move the pontoon train down the river to the vicinity of Campbellton, and watch the river for the return of Gen. McCook. Gen. McCook crossed below Campbellton, about thirty miles from here. At the rate the train moves it will take two days to move to that point.

Israel Garrard,
Col. Seventh Ohio Volunteer Cavalry.

CSA
Atlanta, Ga., August 1, 1864.

Hon. J.A. Seddon,
Secretary of War, Richmond:
On yesterday and the day before our cavalry, under Gens. Wheeler and Jackson, fought near Newnan the raiding party of the enemy which had intercepted our communication with Macon, completely routing them, killing a large number, capturing all their artillery, ambulances, most of their arms and equipments, with a large number of prisoners, including 2 brigade commanders and 12 surgeons, and recapturing all property and prisoners previously taken from us. Major-Gen. Wheeler reports the expedition entirely broken up.

J.B. Hood,
General.

Atlanta, Ga., August 1, 1864.

Hon. James A. Seddon,
Secretary of War, Richmond:
The following dispatch is just received from Brigadier-Gen. Iverson, through Major-Gen. Cobb, at Macon, concerning the party of raiders who struck the Macon and Savannah road:

Gen. Stoneman, after having his force routed, yesterday surrendered with 500 men. The rest of his command are scattered and fleeing toward Eatonton. Many have already been killed or captured. I shall be in Macon today, and wish rations for my men and prisoners.

A. Iverson,
Brigadier-Gen.

J. B. Hood,
General.

FED
Hqtrs. First Cav. Div., Dept. of the Cumberland,
Near Chattahoochee River Railroad Bridge,

August 7, 1864.

General: ...For full particulars of the details of the expedition I refer you to the accompanying reports of brigade and regimental Commanders. A brief summary of results is as follows: Two and a half miles of the Atlanta and West Point Railroad and telegraph destroyed near Palmetto; the same amount of Macon and Western Railroad and five miles of telegraph destroyed at Lovejoy's Station; 1,160 wagons burned, 2,000 mules killed or disabled; 1,000 bales cotton destroyed; 1,000 sacks of corn; 300 sacks of flour, and large quantities of bacon and tobacco...

No serious opposition was met until we commenced our return. Wherever an inferior force of the enemy attempted to retard our advance, we charged through their line. No skirmishing was permitted. After cutting the Macon Railroad at Lovejoy's Station, I found that Gen. Wheeler's command was between me and the point (McDonough) where I had expected to communicate with Gen. Stoneman. After consultation with my brigade commanders, I determined to return to the Chattahoochee by way of Newnan. Two miles from the railroad, Jackson's division attacked us and were repulsed. We then marched toward Newnan, on an obscure road, burning a cavalry supply train (wagons) we met. Near Newnan the railroad and telegraph were cut in three places. At Brown's Mill, between there and the river, I was surrounded by an overwhelming force; Roddy, Wheeler, and Jackson were all there with cavalry, and a large infantry force besides. I attacked at once, hoping to break their line and reach the Franklin Road and the river. In this attack the whole right of their line was broken and demoralized. Ross' Texan brigade was destroyed, all his men and horses captured or killed, and Gen. Ross himself a prisoner; but fresh troops came to fill their places, and after putting every soldier I had into the fight, even to my escort, I found I could not hold the advantage gained, or get through their line in any ordinary manner. I then ordered Col. Croxton, commanding my First Brigade, and Lt. Col. Torrey, commanding my Second Brigade, to cut their way through, strike some road leading south, and endeavor to reach the Chattahoochee at the nearest point and cross... Lt. Col. Jones, Eighth Indiana, with his own regiment, the Fifth Iowa, and a part of the Second Indiana and Fourth Tennessee, remained with me, cut a way through in the midst of a most terrible fire, and crossed the river at Philpot's Ferry, below Franklin. Lt. Miller, commanding a section of the Eighteenth Indiana Battery, by my orders destroyed his guns, caissons, and carriages, cut the harness to pieces, mounted the cannoneers on the artillery horses, and accompanied me. They all got through safely. Col. Brownlow, First Tennessee, and Major Star, Second Kentucky, also brought detachments through....

After crossing the Chattahoochee, I marched to Wedowee, Ala., exchanging our worn-out stock and remounting our dismounted men from the plantations along the road, and would have marched to Talladega, destroyed the iron-works and returned by way of Rome, but for information received in a dispatch, addressed to the rebel Gen. Clanton, which was intercepted by my scouts. I changed my course and returned through Buchanan, Draketown, &c., to Marietta, finding many Union citizens on the route....

I regard the raid as a brilliant success, and had the forces of Gen. Stoneman been able to unite with mine near McDonough, as I understood was contemplated by the Gen. commanding the military division, I think we might have successfully carried our arms wherever desired, and accomplished more magnificent results than any raid in the history of this war....

E.M. McCook,
Brigadier-Gen.,
Commanding Division.

Brig.-Gen. W.L. Elliott,
Chief of Cavalry.

8TH Iowa Cavalry Guidon.

Regimental Reports:

No. 382.

Report of Col. John T. Croxton, Fourth Kentucky Mounted Infantry, Commanding First Brigade, of operations July 27 - 30 (McCook's raid).

Hqtrs. First Brigade, First Cavalry Division,
Kingston, Ga., August 20, 1864.

Captain: ... We moved at once to Smith's Ferry, six miles south of Campbellton, reaching it at daylight, capturing a rebel scout on the western, and finding no force on the eastern, bank of the river. By direction of the Gen. commanding the division, I began crossing the brigade, dismounted in a single bateau, capable of transporting four men, and by 12 n, when the pontoon train arrived, had crossed nearly the whole of my brigade. At 3 p.m. the bridge had been thrown over, and the Second Brigade having crossed and moved in advance on the Palmetto Road, the horses of my command were brought over; the brigade mounted and followed the Second about two miles, when we took a road to the right, the First Tennessee in advance, pressing on rapidly, encountering only a small squad of the enemy, and reaching Palmetto at sundown simultaneously with the Second Brigade. Here we were busily engaged for two hours in destroying the railroad and telegraph line. We then moved, following the Second Brigade, on the Fayetteville Road, reaching that place at daylight on the 29th.

For five miles west of the town the road upon either side was lined with the enemy's (wagon) trains, which were taken possession of by details from the advance brigade. At sunrise we left Fayetteville, my brigade in the advance, on the road to Lovejoy's Station. Col. Brownlow, of the First Tennessee, had the advance, supported by a battalion of the Eighth Iowa, under command of Major Root, until we reached Flint River, four miles from Fayetteville. We continued to find the rebel (wagon) trains. The quartermasters in charge, with the teamsters and guards, were captured by the advance, and the wagons left for the rear guard to burn. A few who had escaped from the train had hurried on and fired the bridge over Flint River, when Col. Brownlow came up and captured the party and saved the bridge.

At 7 a.m. we struck the railroad half a mile north of Lovejoy's Station, and immediately cut the telegraph line and began to destroy the track. Here we remained until 2 p.m., when the command moved back on the road we came, my brigade in the rear, the regiments marching left in front. About a mile from the railroad the column in front had turned square to the left, taking a road that lead in a southwesterly direction toward Newnan. Just as the advance of my brigade reached this road a brigade of rebels appeared in front and began firing on us. I saw it was impossible to get away without fighting, and accordingly ordered Col. Dorr, of the Eighth Iowa, to charge down the road and drive them back and hold them until I could get the other regiments in line. With the advance battalion of his regiment Col. Dorr dashed against the head of the enemy's column, drove it back with confusion, and was only checked by the enemy' troops in rear, which were promptly deployed on either side of the road. It gave me time, however, to get the remainder of the Eighth Iowa and First Tennessee in position, and covering the road we were to hold, I intended the Fourth Kentucky to pass on and take position farther on the road and to cover it while I withdrew the other regiments.

The enemy, however, attacked us immediately with such force and vigor that I found it necessary to put the Fourth Kentucky, except two companies, in on the right of the First Tennessee, which I did, so as to strike the left of the enemy's line in flank. Just at this time an orderly, sent to inform the gen. commanding the division, returned, stating that the enemy were moving on our road between my brigade and the one in advance. I ordered two companies, under Capt. Hudnall, to move up the road, communicate with the column, and hold the road open. At the

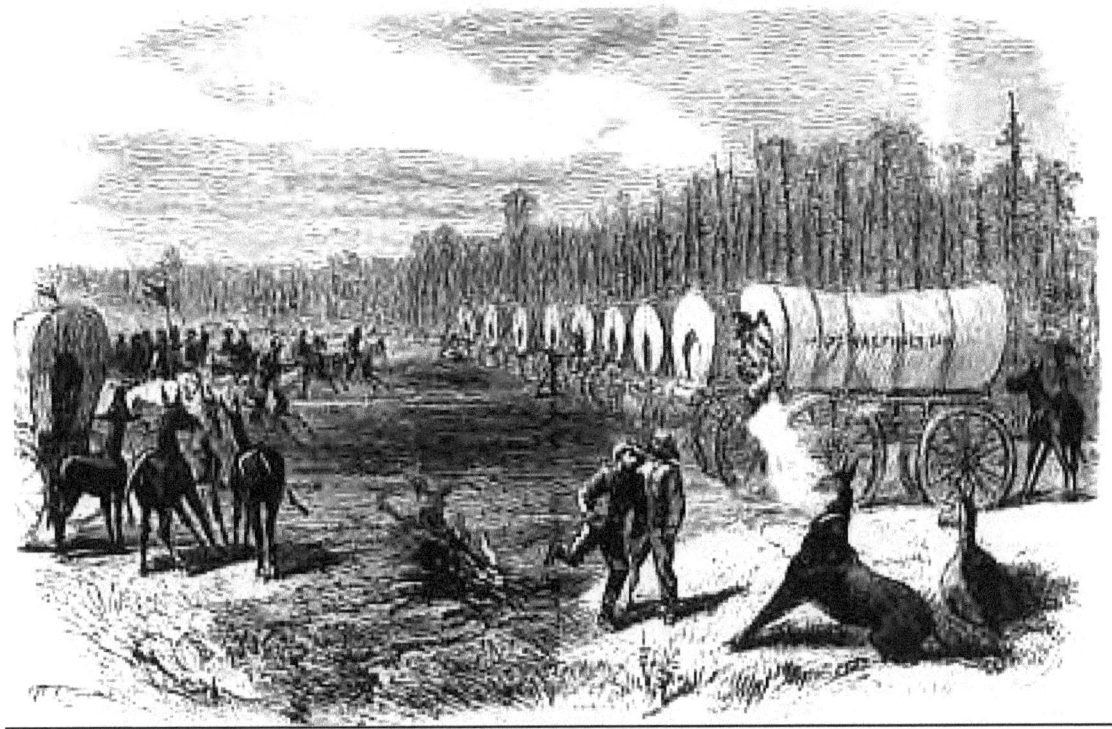

Federal Cavalry capture the supply trains in Fayetteville, burning the wagons and sabering the mules. From the Aug. 13, 1864 Harpers Magazine.

same time I ordered the whole line to move forward and drive the enemy from our front and be ready to withdraw promptly. The line moved and the enemy were driven back, though not without considerable loss to us in killed and wounded. The whole of the brigade was rapidly withdrawn and proceeded on the road... We had galloped on for about seven miles when a messenger from Col. Kelly informed me he had been attacked in rear. The next moment a number of men of the Fourth Kentucky who had escaped, galloped up, reported the regiment completely surrounded, and the enemy pursuing the rest of the brigade...

...At Newnan Col. Harrison's brigade took the rear, and we followed the artillery in rear of the Second Brigade. Several miles southwest of Newnan, the Gen. commanding the division rode back to the head of my brigade, advised me that the enemy were in front and on our right flank...

... In the meantime the enemy was appearing on all sides, and, as for as I could tell, we were completely surrounded. After Col. Harrison's brigade had failed to open the road, I proposed to the General commanding the division that I would take my brigade, or what was left of it, and try and find my way out. He consented, and the regiments were ordered to prepare for the movement...

John T. Croxton,
Col. Fourth Kentucky, Comdg. First Brig., First Div.

Capt. Le Roy,
Asst. Adjutant-Gen., Cavalry Division.

FROM THE DIARY OF JOSIAH CONZETT, 5ᵀᴴ IOWA CAVALRY:

...They remained in camp about two weeks on the north bank of the Chattahoochee River, in front of the Rebel lines and in sight of Atlanta. Sometime towards the last of July, they (our reg.) with 3 others under Gen. Ed McCook were sent on an expedition south, in the rear of the Rebel lines, to cut their communications with their source of supplies and reinforcements. Our regiment was commanded by Maj. Harlon Baird and our company by 1st Lieutenant Andrew Guler. Our valiant Captain and that great 2nd Lieutenant O. A. Langworthy were too tired to go. Only those that had good sound horses were allowed to go. Brother Dave's horse was completely used up so he had to stay back, much against his will. The command had gone but a few miles when Billy Andrews got sick. Dave gladly took his horse, and so he rode out to his death; Billy to camp, safety and home with the rest of us fortunate ones. They rode into the Rebel lines and destroyed mile after mile of railroad tracks, besides a great deal of other property. One day they captured a large wagon train with its guard, teamsters &c. They burned the train and paroled the men. If now they had turned back, all would have been well. They had done all and more they had set out to do and the line of retreat was yet open. But no, fate had ordered it otherwise. They kept on one more day, and then it was too late. A large Rebel force was after them. They now tried another route to try and cut their way out, but on the 30th of July they were brought to bay and to stop and fight. This took place at Newnan, Georgia, 4 miles south of it and about 60 miles south of Atlanta, on the plantation of an old retired Presbyterian Minister by the name of Cook. Here they stopped and fought a greatly superior force for 3 or 4 hours. Our boys had a battery of 3 guns, light field artillery, which they unlimbered right in the rear of said Minister's house (a log one, but quite a comfortable one). The boys made hard use of those guns, they checked several Rebel rushes and no doubt did great damage. They, the Rebels, were hidden from our men, sheltered by heavy brush and timber and seldom showed themselves except when they attempted a charge. But the Gen., seeing that all would be up with them in a short time as they were being hemmed in closer and closer and the last possible chance for retreat cut off, ordered our regiment to dismount and charge them in hopes of gaining a little time to get out to the yet clear road. And right gallantly did the dear old 5th Iowa respond. They scattered the Rebs in that charge far enough to gain time for those that yet had horses to gain the road, and then it was every man for himself. The unhorsed boys took to the brush and tried to escape that way, but only a very few reached camp. The rest were captured, and for months after suffered all the martyrdom of that hell on earth: Andersonville. Quite a number died there, amongst which was Martin Tebbets. A quiet man, but a good soldier and a civil engineer for the ICRR when he enlisted with us in 1861. He was one of our company. In that fatal charge my dear brother Dave was instantly killed by being shot in the head. He died as he said he would like to if he had to die: a soldiers death on the field. In coming back from that charge most of the men saw him lying there. One of them, Horton, was brave and thoughtful enough to stop and take his revolver to bring to me. But as he had lost his horse, he saw the chances of getting away very poor. He gave it to Henry Sauer, who was on horseback, telling him to give it to me with the particulars, which he did, for he got to our lines in safety. The most foolish thing I ever did, and shall always regret, was that I did not keep it and bring it home, but turned it over to the government.

Lieutenant Guler had also lost his horse, so he with 3 or 4 of the boys took to the woods. They were striking out in the direction of our army when they were suddenly confronted by a squad of Rebels who at once demanded their surrender. All the boys surrendered except Lieut. Guler. He refused and showed fight and he was instantly killed. Guler was a good man and a brave soldier. He was not brilliant, but was well liked by the company and very popular at home. No one knows where his grave is, as he was left where he fell. He probably fills one of the many graves marked unknown. The only one in that party that escaped was Oscar Martin. He dropped behind a log when the Rebs shot, crept in the bushes unnoticed and, after the party marched off, struck into the woods and was off wandering around a week or 10 days. Protected, fed and guided, he finally reached Marietta, Ga. without hardly any clothes, hat or shoes, but oh, so happy...

No. 383.

Reports of Col. James P. Brownlow, First Tennessee Cavalry, commanding First Brigade, of operations July 27 - 31 (McCook's raid).

Hqtrs. First Cav. Div., Dept. of the Cumberland,

Marietta, Ga., August 1, 1864.

General: ...On the 30th we moved in the direction of Newnan, with a view of recrossing the river at Moore's Bridge. Here we were attacked at 8 a.m. by two divisions of cavalry and one division of infantry. The fighting was desperate during the entire day. At 5 p.m., seeing that the division would be overwhelmed and compelled to surrender, Gen. McCook gave permission to the commanding officers to save themselves, if possible. I cut the enemy's lines with 600 men, but was unable to cross more than 150 on account of the enemy's crossing in force at Moore's Bridge...

Jas. P. Brownlow,
Col. Commanding.

Brig.-Gen. W.L. Elliott,
Chief of Cavalry.

No. 391.

Reports of Capt. Lewis M.B. Smith, First Wisconsin Cavalry.

Hqtrs. First Wisconsin Cavalry,
Cartersville, Ga., September 6, 1864.

...July 28, recrossed the river six miles below Campbellton; regiment detached, proceeded to Campbellton; two and a half miles east of the place, on the Fairburn Road, attacked the advance of Gen. Armstrong's division, 2,000 strong, and after a severe fight withdrew, losing Major Paine, commanding regiment, killed; Lt. Warren and 9 men killed, wounded, and missing; returned to Marietta, July 31, escorting pontoon train and battery...

Capt. L.M.B. Smith,
First Wisconsin Cavalry.

FROM THE HISTORY OF THE 8TH IOWA CAVALRY

On the 29th the command reached Lovejoy where the railroad was torn up and obstructed, after which the retreat began. Soon after a fierce attack was made on the Union army and a severe battle took place. The Eighth Cavalry bore a

The 8th Iowa Cavalry. Col. Dorr is lower middle with the moustache.

conspicuous part, losing between twenty and thirty men, killed or wounded. Among the killed were Lieutenants James Horton and Joseph H. Cobb, both gallant young officers who fell at the head of the column. Colonel Dorr and many others were wounded. On the next day the Battle of Newman was fought with a largely superior force of the enemy. As the head of our column entered Newman it encountered Rhoddy's dismounted cavalry, which was soon after reinforced by Wheeler and a fierce battle ensued. Croxton's Brigade, in which was the Eight Iowa, at once made a gallant charge on the enemy's lines, forcing them to give way but the rest of the division failed to come up in time so that the Confederates rallied and held their position. The fight was continued for some time by the First Brigade alone, now commanded by Dorr. This enabled most of the command to reach the main army in safety while Colonel Dorr with his regiment was captured by the enemy. They had made a most gallant fight against vastly superior numbers and only surrendered when further resistance was hopeless. Of the three hundred and sixteen officers and men who started on the raid but twenty ever regained the Union lines. After some months' imprisonment Colonel Dorr and a portion of his men were exchanged and rejoined the army then resisting Hood's invasion.

No. 396.

Report of Lt. Wm. B. Rippetoe, Eighteenth Indiana Battery.

Hqtrs. Eighteenth Indiana Battery,
Sandtown, Ga., September 10, 1864.

...July 27, crossed the Chattahoochee River at Mason's Ferry and proceeded to Smith's Ferry, where the battery was put in position covering the laying of a pontoon bridge. One section, commanded by Lt. Miller, went with Gen. McCook on a raid to cut the Macon Road. July 29, four guns returned to Marietta, arriving there the night of the 30th.

...August 5, Lt. Miller returned and reported the loss of his section. The carriages were cut down and the harness destroyed by order of Gen. McCook, after the ammunition was all expended...

Wm. B. Rippetoe,
First Lieutenant Eighteenth Indiana Battery, Commanding.

Brigadier-Gen. Brannan,
Chief of Artillery, Dept. of the Cumberland.

No. 444.

Report of Capt. Wm. Kossak, Aide-de-Camp, in charge of pontoon train.

Pontoon Train, Dept. of the Tennessee,
Camp near Atlanta, Ga., September 10, 1864.

...On the morning of July 27, I received orders from Brig.Gen. E.M. McCook to dismantle and join his cavalry command. This was accomplished at once, pickets ferried back to the command, and the line of march taken across Nickajack and Sweet Water in the direction of Campbellton. On this march the extreme heaviness of this pontoon train and the miserable condition of the mules proved a serious drawback on the celerity and dispatch of this cavalry movement. The march lasted until 2 a.m. next morning, July 28, during which time I lost 18 mules, dropping dead in their harness. When the command arrived opposite Campbellton, after a consultation with me, Gen. McCook concluded not to bridge the river at Campbellton, on account of the unfavorable, and it was concluded to continue the march to Riverton, seven miles farther downstream. It was impossible to take the whole train along, on account of the condition of the draft animals. I took, therefore, only enough material for one bridge along, and left the remainder back, guarded by one battalion of cavalry and two pieces. Traveling at a brisk rate, by 2 p.m. the pickets were ferried across and deployed, the bridge thrown, and Gen. McCook and his whole command crossed it. To lose no time nobody dismounted, but the command went over in solid column, and the bridge stood it well. Under protection of Col. Hamilton, with the Ninth Ohio Cavalry and two pieces, the bridge remained on water till noon July 29, when it was taken up and loaded, and started, under the escort of Col. Hamilton and his command, back. We passed Campbellton safely, from which place the enemy fired both times a few random shots, and joined that portion of the bridge that was left behind. The whole train arrived on July 31 safely at Pace's Ferry, Chattahoochee River, near Vining's Station, and went into camp...

Capt. Wm. Kossak,
Aide-de-Camp.

CHAPTER 4 AUGUST 3 - SEPTEMBER 1

The losses at Newnan and Clinton shook Sherman. He confided to Gen. Halleck *"...1 can hardly believe it, as he (McCook) had 3000 picked cavalry. The loss of this cavalry is a serious one to me (8-1-64)..."* He began immediately to look for replacements as far away as St. Louis. He needed horses and men to protect his flanks and rear area. As would be expected, reports came in that Confederate Gen. Wheeler and much of his cavalry force had crossed the river below Campbellton and were heading north behind Sherman's line of march. His fears were realized as Wheeler retook Dalton, on the railroad between Chattanooga and Atlanta.

The Federals immediately moved Gen. Kilpatrick's cavalry from Cartersville to the Chattahoochee River:

Proceed with your division to Chattahoochee River, taking the Sandtown Road. Should you find any stragglers from First Division (McCook's), bring them up with you...(Gen. Elliot 8-1-64).

Gen. Judson Kilpatrick at his headquarters tent.

Gen. Kilpatrick moved in to replace Stoneman and McCooks battered units, most of whom were sent out of the fighting around Atlanta. One unit of Stoneman's brigades, the 7th Pennsylvania and the 9th Michigan, under Col. Israel Garrard, were

KILPATRICK AND COL. ISRAEL GARRARD AT SANDTOWN AUGUST 11-15

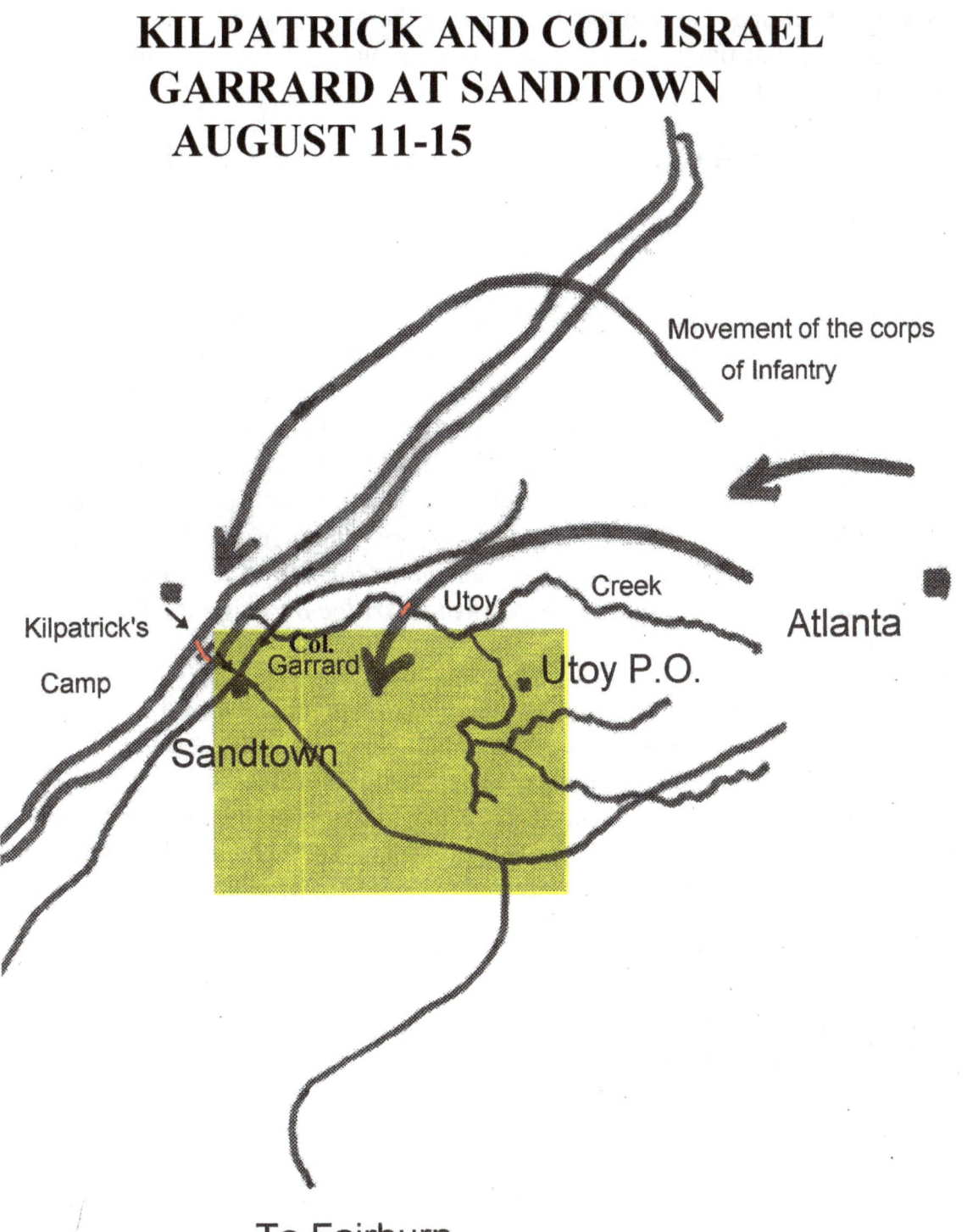

sent to shore up the defenses of Utoy Creek. Fear that Confederate cavalry would attempt to cut the railroad at Vinings by crossing the Utoy was rife. As soon as Sherman was sure that flank was safe, he devised a plan to feint a crossing at Sandtown to see what strength the enemy had south of Utoy Creek.

FIELDER JONES AT CAMPBELLTON, AUGUST 8TH

In David Evan's epic *Sherman's Horsemen,* he discusses another ruse employed by Sherman:

To further the illusion a crossing was imminent, Fielder Jones's 2nd Brigade left Sweet Water Bridge that morning with three days' rations and the remaining section of the 10th Wisconsin Battery. Striking the Chattahoochee opposite Campbellton, Jones's men began banging away while the Wisconsin battery's 3-inch rifles lobbed shells across the river. They kept up this charade until just before dark, when Jones had his men build campfires in the woods to make it look like a large force had moved down to the river. The brigade then quietly moved upstream, crossed the mouth of Sweetwater Creek, and camped near Alexander's Mill before returning to Sweetwater Bridge on August 10th.

At this point it became clear to all that the Confederates had no appreciable cavalry forces west of Atlanta. This presented Sherman with a plan. He would defend everything north of Utoy Creek, have Kilpatrick make a demonstration, as if to cross at Sandtown Ferry and see what happens. Seeing no response from the enemy, he sent Col. Israel Garrard across the Utoy in force, on the 10th of August. When little opposition appeared, Sherman shared his plan *"...1 have just ordered Garrard and Kilpatrick to take advantage of the absence of Wheeler to strike the enemy's flanks (to McCook 8-14-64)..."*

On the 15th, Kilpatrick and his cavalry crossed the Chattahoochee at the Sandtown Ferry and set out for Fairburn, where they destroyed the rails coming west out of Atlanta. Though Gen. Armstrong's Confederates were in the vicinity, they did not engage Kilpatrick. The next day, Sherman ordered his entire Army to the right, to cross Utoy Creek and link up with the cavalry movement:

General Kilpatrick's cavalry will move to Camp Creek; Gen. Schofield will cover the Campbellton Road. ..The Army of the Tennessee will withdraw, cross Utoy Creek, and move by the most direct road toward Fairburn, going as far as Camp Creek... The Armies of the Ohio and Tennessee will move direct for the West Point Road, aiming to strike it between Red Oak and Fairburn...Gen. Kilpatrick will act as the advance and Gen. Garrard will cover the rear.. .The bridges at

Sandtown will be kept and protected by a detachment of cavalry detailed by Gen. Elliott, with a section of guns or four gun battery and communication kept up with the army as far as possible by way of Sandtown...

A SAD STORY FROM SANDTOWN

The Reverend Henley Campbell of Owl Rock Church was well known in these parts for the many stories of the early days of Campbell County. One of the saddest was that of a boy who was a Confederate sharpshooter at Sandtown. When Garrard crossed the Utoy on August 10th, the Federal cavalry met little resistance. Most of the pickets skedaddled, except one 16 year old boy. He was dressed in mere rags, a terrible sight for even the enemy to see. He had his musket confiscated and was taken before Garrard's staff and questioned.

After cursory interrogation, the officers asked him to empty his pockets. From his left pocket he pulled a handful of long sticks. From his right pocket came a number of short sticks. He was asked what the devil these sticks were doing in his pocket. He replied, saying the long sticks were enlisted men and the short sticks, officers.

There he stood, ragged, a young boy unable to lie to his captures. He had shot a great number of Federal soldiers and it incensed Garrard's men. After a drum head trial, he was hanged at the Sandtown crossroads.

The Confederates began immediately to see the movement; infantry appeared between Campbellton and Sandtown and fortifications were thrown up on Sweetwater Creek. The latter were placed on the east side at Jones Ferry crossing and can still be seen today.

On the 28th, Hood sent the news to Secretay of War Seddon, indicating that "*the enemy have changed their entire position, the left of their line resting near the Chattahoochee about Sandtown and their right extending to a point opposite and near the West Point Railroad between East Point and Fairburn...*"

The Federal armies poured over Utoy Creek and the crossing at Sandtown. One arm of the force destroyed the Atlanta and West Point railroad for miles and camped there on the tracks, daring Hood to chase them off. Another force converged on the Macon Railroad about Jonesboro, where a final battle for Atlanta took place. When the West Point and Griffin Roads were destroyed, Gen. Hood had no choice but to abandon Atlanta.

OFFICIAL REPORTS AUGUST 3 - SEPTEMBER 1:

Near Atlanta, Ga., August 3, 1864 11:30 p.m.

Maj.-Gen. H.W. Halleck,
Washington, D.C.:
In order to make my campaign conclusive I should have a large cavalry force. We find great difficulty in procuring horses. I understand there are 2,000 at St. Louis. Can I have them. Recruits should also be sent to Nashville, and sent forward daily, and distributed as they come.

W.T. Sherman,
Major-Gen.

Hqtrs. Military Division of the Mississippi,
In the field, near Atlanta, Ga., August 3, 1864.

Gen. Webster,
Nashville:
Gen. McCook is safe. He is in with 1200 of his command. About 500 had got into Marietta before him. Still I will need cavalry.

W.T. Sherman,
Major-Gen.

Nashville, August 3, 1864.

Major-Gen. Sherman:
Lewis Merrill, chief of Cavalry Bureau at St. Louis, telegraphs me he has 2,000 cavalry horses on hand, and will send them to me if they will allow it at Washington. This in reply to a telegram from me. They might give you 1,000 of these animals if you request it, if not all. They will deny me. I have asked too often.

J.L. Donaldson,
Sr. and Supervising Quartermaster.

Hqtrs. Chief of Cavalry, Dept. of the Cumberland,
August 3, 1864.

Gen. J. Kilpatrick,
Cartersville, or en route to Marietta, Ga.:
I have reports that 500 to 1,000 rebels crossed Chattahoochee at Campbellton last night and moved in direction of Burnt Hickory. Look out for them on railroad.

W.L. Elliott,
Brig.-Gen. and Chief of Cavalry.

Special Field Orders, No. 52.
Hqtrs. Mil. Div. of the Mississippi,
In the field near Atlanta, Ga.,
August 5, 1864.

I. Brig.-Gen. John McArthur is hereby assigned to the command of the district of country embracing Kennesaw, Marietta, Roswell, and the west bank of the Chattahoochee River and the Sweet Water...

L.M. Dayton,
Aide-de-Camp.

Hqtrs. Dept. of the Cumberland,
August 7, 1864 - 8:30 p.m.

Major-Gen. Sherman:
The guns have been ordered by express train with ammunition, and I will look up the best position for them tomorrow. Have directed Elliott to make arrangements for the distribution of the horses. He thinks he can bring up McCook's division to about 3,000. McCook's men are constantly coming in and Kilpatrick reports that he has taken some prisoners, rebel cavalry, near Campbellton. The enemy still occupies his entrenchments in my front in considerable force.

Geo. H. Thomas,
Major-Gen., U.S. Volunteers, Commanding.

Hqtrs. Military Division of the Mississippi,
In the field, near Atlanta, August 8, 1864.

Gen. Thomas:
The enemy's cavalry manifests activity on our right, threatening to cross Utoy Creek to Gen. Schofield's rear. He has little or no cavalry. I want him tomorrow to develop well the enemy's flank, which I believe is along the south fork of Utoy Creek, covering East Point. To enable him to do this I want a general connonading, the 4 1/2 guns included, if they come in time; and I want you to order Gen. Garrard to send a brigade out to and beyond Decatur on your left, and let Gen. Kilpatrick move down to Sandtown and feign as though intending to cross over. Send orders for him tonight, that the effect may be felt as early in the day as possible. I cannot move Gen. Schofield with any activity as long as that cavalry hovers on his right and rear. We are now as much extended as possible, and must test the strength of our flanks and line.

W. T. Sherman,
Major-Gen., Commanding.

Hqtrs. Military Division of the Mississippi,
In the field, near Atlanta, Ga.,
August 8, 1864.

Gen. Schofield:
Gen. Thomas says that Kilpatrick is at the junction of the Sandtown and Powder Springs roads. I have ordered him to send instructions for him to move down to Sandtown and feign as though crossing. This will engage their attention and I don't believe the enemy will put any considerable cavalry force above Utoy Creek. I think Garrard below the forks (of Utoy) and a brigade of infantry down the Sandtown Road, near Utoy Post-Office, will make that flank perfect.

W.T. Sherman,
Major-Gen., Commanding.

Hqtrs. Military Division of the Mississippi,
In the field, near Atlanta,

August 9, 1864.

Gen. Schofield:
If you have a good cavalry brigadier I will give you Col. Hamilton's regiment, Ninth Ohio, with a full regiment and nearly 500 horses to make a brigade of cavalry, but I must have a real head, one that will give it personal attention.

W.T. Sherman,
Major-Gen., Commanding.

Col. Silas Adams of the 1st Kentucky Cavalry, Ballentine's Brigade.

Schofield's Hqtrs., August 9, 1864.

Major-Gen. Sherman:
I have no good cavalry commander. Col. Adams is probably the best I have. Can you not assign one from some other department? It is very important now for me to have a good man to collect my scattered fragments and bring them into serviceable shape.

J.M. Schofield,
Major-General.

Hqtrs. Military Division of the Mississippi,
In the field, near Atlanta, August 9, 1864.

Gen. Schofield:
I have no cavalry commander at all. All the cavalry of the old Army of the Tennessee is back in Mississippi, and Gen. Thomas' cavalry is not well commanded. Col. Adams told me his time was out, and he was going back to Kentucky to reorganize. You must secure his horses and appraise them, as they belong to the men. Col. Capron is back, how is he?

W.T. Sherman,
Major-Gen., Commanding.

Hqtrs. Army of the Ohio,
Near Atlanta, Ga., August 9, 1864.

Major-Gen. Sherman:
I don't know Col. Capron personally, but understand he is not of much account. Col. Garrard is the best man I have, but he is wanting in dash. I have ordered the appraisal of Col. Adams' horses, and will try to get my cavalry in shape as soon as possible. I cannot do better for the present than to put Col. Garrard in command, unless Col. Hamilton is better. I know nothing of him.

J.M. Schofield,
Major-Gen.

Sherman's Hqtrs.,August 10, 1864.
(Received 10:55 p.m.)

Gen. Schofield:
I will come down tomorrow and go with you to Hascall's position. I suppose Hamilton's regiment of cavalry has reported to you. Kilpatrick is on the opposite bank at Sandtown. Order Col. Garrard tomorrow to replace his bridge over Utoy and feel across to the south bank of the creek.

W.T. Sherman,
Major-Gen.

Hqtrs. Army of the Ohio,
August 11, 1864 - 8:30 p.m.

Major-Gen. Sherman:
Col. Garrard has returned from his scout. He crossed the Utoy Creek at the bridge, and went as far as Sandtown; thence toward Atlanta two miles and a half, and to the Owl Rock Church and across the right of Gen. Hascall's position. He found only cavalry pickets on any of the roads. The large cavalry camps appeared to be a day or two old. Citizens informed him that Armstrong's division - three brigades - had camped near the church night before last and started for Campbellton yesterday morning, saying they were going on a raid. Gen. Kilpatrick had shelled Sandtown day before yesterday, but none of his troops were in sight today.

J.M. Schofield,
Major-Gen.

Hqtrs. Military Division of the Mississippi,
In the field, near Atlanta, August 11, 1864.

Gen. Schofield:
Dispatch received. Am glad to hear that Col. Garrard has connected Sandtown with Gen. Hascall's position. Armstrong will not make a raid on us from the direction of Campbellton. Gen. Kilpatrick can whip his division if he crosses the Chattahoochee.

W.T. Sherman,
Major-Gen., Commanding.

Hqtrs. Cavalry Command, Dept. of the Ohio,
Before Atlanta, Ga., August 11, 1864.

Major J.A. Campbell,
Asst. Adjutant-Gen.:
Major: I have the honor to report that, under the orders of last night to scout the country south of Utoy Creek, I took 450 men of the Ninth Michigan Cavalry, Seventh Ohio Cavalry, and the Ninth Illinois Mounted Infantry, and crossed Utoy Creek at the bridge. Rebel vedettes were found not far from the bridge, and again at Sandtown. There was a picket-post near Sandtown, on the Fayetteville Road; when driven from it they retreated southward. He showed but a small force, and there appeared to be no reinforcement of the rebel picket. I concluded that it was a post of observation only. Gen. Kilpatrick had shelled Sandtown day before yesterday, but there were none of his troops in sight from Sandtown. I then took the road from Sandtown to Atlanta and returned on it two miles and a half to the road that leads to Owl Rock Church. I made a scout out on this to the camp-ground. Many fires of a large camp were still smoking. A respectable citizen, an old man, Mr. McWilliams, who lives near the church, stated that Armstrong's division of three brigades had camped there night before last, and had left there yesterday morning on the road toward Campbellton, saying they were going on a raid...A number of picket-posts at cross-roads on the Sandtown Road were found, but the corn blades were two days or more old. It was evident that the cavalry had been moved out of that part of the country...

Israel Garrard,
Col., Commanding.

Hqtrs. Military Division of the Mississippi.
In the field, near Atlanta,
August 11, 1864.

Gen. Howard:
The transfer of the Ninth Ohio was made permanent, at Col. Hamilton's representation that he belonged to no brigade and had 400 men. Gen. Schofield having lost Gen. Stoneman needs cavalry on his flank. We must put our joint shoulders to the wheel and scrape up all the horses we can, else the enemy will ride all around and over us.

W.T. Sherman,
Major-Gen., Commanding.

Col. Israel Garrard

Hqtrs. Army of the Cumberland,
August 13, 1864.

Major-Gen. Sherman:
Garrard has already received his orders to scout as far as Roswell. He sent a scouting party some distance beyond Decatur, both south and in the direction of Covington, yesterday, but discovered nothing. Have sent orders for Kilpatrick to put down the bridge at Sandtown.

Geo. H. Thomas.
Major-Gen., U.S. Volunteers, Commanding.

Proposition:
Hqtrs. Dept. and Army of the Tenn.,
Before Atlanta, Ga., August 13, 1864.

Accumulate all impedimenta not going at proposed depot prior to movement, and move trains of Armies of the Ohio and the Cumberland, under cover as much as possible, to vicinity of Utoy Creek, there to be parked and guarded by infantry: this the day before the troops draw out. Then:

First: Move fourth Corps in the night to position in rear of Fourteenth Corps, so that the Twentieth Corps can withdraw at daylight and march to proposed depot, cavalry following closely Twentieth Corps, and taking up position on the south side of Proctor's Creek. Next night let trains of Army of the Tennessee move down Green's Ferry Road, under guard, toward Sandtown, and park near Utoy Creek.

Second: At daylight Armies of the Ohio and the Cumberland move out simultaneously, by two routes if possible, in the direction of Fairburn, Army of the Ohio to halt in position. Army of the Cumberland to form on it's left, and the Army of the Tennessee, marching at the same hour, to pass via Utoy or Sandtown to the rear and right of the other two armies. The three armies will march by three roads if possible, not more than two miles apart. The cavalry (Kilpatrick's) intended to cover the right flank to precede the Army of the Ohio, and that intended for the left flank to follow the Army of the Tennessee as far as Utoy Creek.

O.O. Howard,
Major-Gen.

CSA
Circular:
Hqtrs. Lee's Corps, Phillip's House,
August 13, 1864.

It has been reported to these headquarters that, contrary to orders, intercourse between our pickets and those of the enemy is still kept up, and in some instances it has been agreed that they shall not fire at each other with intent to kill, but to shoot over each others' heads. A stop must be put to these proceedings, and anyone found so offending will be sent to these headquarters. Artillery officers and men in the trenches are directed to fire upon any man, or group of men, who are discovered holding communication with the enemy.
By command of Lt.-Gen. Lee:

J.W. Ratchford,
Asst. Adjutant-Gen.

FED
Hqtrs. Military Division of the Mississippi,
In the field, near Atlanta, Ga.,
August 14, 1864.

Gen. Thomas:
Gen. McArthur, at Marietta, reports small bodies of cavalry approach Marietta from the northeast. Gen. Garrard should send frequently (sic) up to Roswell and McAfee's. You may order Gen. Kilpatrick to lay down a bridge at Sandtown, and be prepared to scour the country down as far as Camp Creek.

W.T. Sherman,
Major-Gen., Commanding.

Sherman's Hqtrs.,
August 14, 1864.

Gen. McCook:
Cannot John E. Smith's infantry drive that brigade at Fairmount? I think that Steedman at Chattanooga will come out and meet Wheeler at or near Dalton. I have just ordered Garrard and Kilpatrick to take advantage of the absence of Wheeler to strike the enemy's flanks. Collect your men and be ready to catch detachments of Wheeler on their return.

W.T. Sherman,
Major-Gen.

Hqtrs. Military Division of the Mississippi,
In the field, near Atlanta,
August 14, 1864 (Received 8:45 p.m.)

Gen. Schofield:
There is no doubt Wheeler is up about Dalton with a large cavalry force. I want our cavalry now to feel the enemy's flanks strong, and will order Gen. Kilpatrick to cross at Sandtown and make a bold push for Fairburn, and Gen. Garrard in like manner to feel well round the enemy's right flank. Let your cavalry go down in the morning to Sandtown and report for the expedition to Gen. Kilpatrick.
W.T. Sherman,

Major-Gen., Commanding.

Hqtrs. Chief of Cavalry, Dept. of the Cumberland,
August 14, 1864.

Brigadier-Gen. J. Kilpatrick,
Commanding Third Cavalry Division:
The Gen. commanding directs that you cross the Chattahoochee, fortify the position at the bridge, and scout and clear the country of rebels to Camp Creek. Your train will be kept at the railroad bridge until your position on the south side is securely established.

David F. How,
Lt. and acting Asst. Adjutant-Gen.

The Vinings railroad bridge, rebuilt in August in only 4 and ½ days.

Hqtrs. Chief of Cavalry, Dept. of the Cumberland,
August 14, 1864.

Gen. Kilpatrick:
You will make a bold reconnaissance in the direction of Fairburn to railroad if you can reach it. It is reported that Wheeler with 6,000 cavalry and artillery has gone north. If true, you will have only Jackson's cavalry to contend with. If the opportunity offers try to break him up. Gen. Schofield's small force of cavalry will be ordered to cooperate with you. It is on the south side of Utoy Creek, and will report to you at Sandtown tomorrow.

W.L. Elliott,
Brigadier-Gen. and Chief of Cavalry.

Hqtrs. Dept. of the Cumberland,
August 16, 1864.

Major-Gen. Sherman:
The following received from Kilpatrick, dated August 15, 9 p.m., near Camp Creek, en route from Fairburn:

Thus far my reconnaissance has been a success. I crossed the river at 11 A.M., and passed out at once for Fairburn. I forced the enemy back into his camp near railroad, five miles above the station. Destroyed the station, public buildings, telegraph and railroad for about three miles. Jackson's division of cavalry has thus far refused to give me battle. I rather expect an attempt will be made in the morning to prevent my return. They will give me the opportunity I seek to destroy Jackson and his command, provided his cavalry alone meets me...

W.L. Elliott,
Brigadier-Gen. and Chief of Cavalry.

Special Field Orders No. 57.
Hqtrs. Mil. Div. of the Miss.,
In the field, near Atlanta,
August 16, 1864.

The movement of the army against the Macon railroad will begin Thursday night, August 18, and will be continued on the following general plan:

1. All army commanders will send across the Chattahoochee River and within the old rebel works at the bridge and down as far as Turner's Ferry all surplus wagons, horses, men and materials not absolutely neccessary to the success of the expedition, and will collect in their wagons with best teams bread, meat, sugar, coffee, &c., for fifteen days after the 19th instant, and ammunition, and park them near Utoy Creek.
First move: Gen. Kilpatrick's cavalry will move to Camp Creek; Gen. Schofield will cover the Campbellton Road, and Gen. Thomas will move one corps (Gen. Williams) to the Chattahoochee bridge, with orders to hold it, Pace's Ferry Bridge,

and a pontoon bridge (Capt. Kossak's), at Turner's Ferry, ready to be laid down if neccessary. The other Corps, Gen. Stanley's, will move south of Proctor's Creek to near the Utoy, behind the right center of the Army of the Tennessee, prepared to cover the Bell's Ferry Road. Gen. Garrard's cavalry will fall behind Peach Tree Creek, and act against the enemy should he sally against Gen. Williams' or Gen. Stanley's corps during the movement.

Second move: The Army of the Tennessee will withdraw, cross Utoy Creek, and move by the most direct road toward Fairburn, going as far as Camp Creek. Gen. Thomas will mass his two corps, Gens. Stanley's and Johnson's, below Utoy Creek, and Gen. Garrard's cavalry will join Gen. Thomas by the most direct road or by way of Sandtown Bridge, and act with him during the rest of the move. Gen. Schofield will advance abreast of and in communication with the Army of the Tennessee as far as Camp Creek.

Third move: The Armies of the Ohio and Tennessee will move direct for the West Point Road, aiming to strike it between Red Oak and Fairburn. Gen. Thomas will follow well closed up in two columns, the two trains between. Gen. Kilpatrick will act as the advance, and Gen. Garrard will cover the rear, under direction of Gen. Thomas. The bridges at Sandtown will be kept and protected by a detachment of cavalry detailed by Gen. Elliott, with a section of guns or four-gun battery.

II. During the movement, and until the army returns to the river, the utmost care will be taken to expose as little as possible the trains of cars and wagons. The depots at the bridge at Allatoona, and Marietta will be held against any attack, and communication kept up with the army as far as possible by way of Sandtown. On reaching any railroad, the troops will at once be disposed for defense, and at least one-third put to work to tear up track and destroy iron, ties, and all railroad materials.

By order of Major-Gen. Sherman:

L.M. Dayton,
Aide-de-Camp.

CSA
Atlanta, August 16, 1864 - 2 p.m.

Governor J.E. Brown,
Milledgeville, Ga.:
Gen. Wright has been directed to hold the militia at present, as the enemy seems to be threatening a raid on our left from the direction of Campbellton. Can you not replace the men at Andersonville with militia from some quarter of the State other than that?

J.B. Hood,
General.

Hqtrs. Picket,
August 16, 1864.

Capt. Moore:
This morning the enemy's fortifications are plainly visible on the Campbellton Road as far down as the house next below Herron's. Their skirmish line was advanced in the night to the hollow and woods this side Campbellton Road. Their works are well built, and regular fortifications with rifle-pits in front. No movement in front.

J.J. Perry,
Major.

August 17, 1864 - 3:20 p.m.

Brigadier-Gen. Jackson,
Commanding cavalry, &c.:
Gen. Hood is anxious to know what the enemy means by fortifying on the other side of the river - on the Sweet Water. Please instruct your scouts to give their attention to this.

F.A. Shoup,
Chief of Staff.

Hqtrs. Jackson's Cavalry Division,

August 18, 1864 - 2:30 p.m.

Major-Gen. Cleburne:
General: Gen. Armstrong reports at 12 m. that the enemy had driven Col. Pinson, First Mississippi, back to the forks of the road, and were pressing him in strong force. Gen. Ross' scouts report the enemy, both infantry and cavalry, to be at Sandtown and Campbellton, and fortified, but no demonstration of an advance visible.

By order of Brigadier-Gen. W.H. Jackson:

E.T. Sykes,
Asst. Adjutant-Gen.

COL. R. A. PINSON.
FIRST MISSISSIPPI CAVALRY.

The 1st Mississippi Cavalry from a very worn out print (color by Richard Downs).

FED.
Hqtrs. Military Division of the Mississippi,
In the field, near Atlanta,
August 23, 1864 - 7:30 p.m.

Gen. Thomas:
Have your signal corps provided with rockets, and agree on signals by rockets or signal smoke for a few simple messages such as "all well," "send boats to Campbellton," "send a brigade, division or regiment to Campbellton," also "look out for us at Roswell." These signals may be of use to us when we get beyond safe distance for couriers via Sandtown.

W.T. Sherman,
Major-Gen., Commanding.

CSA
Hqtrs. Ross' Brigade, Jackson's Cavalry Division,
Isaac Cook's, Ga., August 27, 1864 - 6 p.m.

Brigadier-Gen. Armstrong,
Commanding Division:
General: My scouts have just reported from the north side of the Chattahoochee. Kilpatrick's is encamped along Sweet Water from Sandtown up. They finished the bridge over the river at Sandtown Monday and took out their pontoons. The advance of enemy on Sandtown and Fayetteville Road is one mile this side of Stephen's house. No farther advance on part of the force on Camp Creek. They are now shelling my pickets.

L.S. Ross,
Brigadier-Gen.

Atlanta, Ga.,
August 28, 1864.

Hon. J.A. Seddon,
Richmond, Va.:
The enemy have changed their entire position, the left of their line resting near the Chattahoochee about Sandtown, and their right extending to a point opposite and

near the West Point railroad between East Point and Fairburn. They hold all the crossings on the Chattahoochee from Pace's Ferry down to Sandtown, but not with a continuous line. Dispatches from Gen. Wheeler of the 19th, in which he reports the capture of Dalton, with large quantity of stores, about 200 prisoners and 200 mules, destroying 3 trains of cars and 25 miles of railroad. His command is in good condition.

J.B. Hood,
General.

August 31, 1864.

Major-Gen. Wheeler,
Commanding Cavalry:
Sherman faces Atlanta from the west, crossing the Chattahoochee at Sandtown. His wagon trains must be greatly exposed. Gen. Hood thinks you had better move this way, destroying as you come, to operate upon them.

F.A. Shoup,
Chief of Staff.

FED
Hqtrs. Fourth Army Corps,
Near Lovejoy's, September 3, 1864.

Gen. Kimball:
General: Official information has just been received from Major-Gen. Sherman that we have Atlanta. On the night of September 1 Hood abandoned the city, and retreated with the force he had there. He destroyed 80 railroad cars of ammunition, blew up the magazines at Atlanta, and destroyed his siege guns. Gen. Slocum occupies the city. A large amount of rebel public property was destroyed. Please have this information published to your regiments.

By order of Major-Gen. Stanley:
Wm. H. Sinclair, Asst. Adjutant-Gen.

The Opposing Lines After September 1, 1864.

Where Hood destroyed train cars of powder and ammunition, only car wheels and track remain.

CHAPTER 5 SEPTEMBER 1 - OCTOBER 1

After the Confederate loss of Atlanta, the campaign entered a strange phase. The Federal armies camped on the railroad tracks leading into Atlanta from the South and west. Sherman ordered a large portion of his infantry in each corps to spend its time destroying rails by heating and twisting them into "Sherman's neckties." He also ordered all civilians to leave Atlanta and negotiated with its mayor, offering transportation for them at Lovejoy Station.

Meanwhile, Gen. Hood's army took up a considerable amount of track from the southern and western rails for iron for horseshoes and the like. The army began to move south and then west, stopping and fortifying at Palmetto, where supplies could still come by rail from West Point, Ga. He sent cavalry east toward Fairburn and Campbellton to picket while his infantry built trench lines along the road from Palmetto to Rivertown. He intended to spend his time reorganizing the Army of Tennessee, whose strength had fallen from a high of 90,000 at the beginning of the campaign, to about 42,000. Governor Brown, incensed at the loss of Atlanta, had ordered his 10,000 Ga. Militia troops to return to their homes.

Gen. Sherman only had a vague idea of Hood's whereabouts and no idea of what he was up to. His plans for a march to the sea, relying only on forage for his supplies, could not be undertaken while a large standing army was in the vicinity. He sent cavalry scouts in all directions looking for the enemy and received many reports of Confederate cavalry attacking in his rear as far north as Dalton and Cartersville. By month's end he would have a better idea of his foes intentions.

On September 26th, President Jefferson Davis arrived in Palmetto to meet with Hood and give his men a pep talk. Federal spies, ever among the Confederates throughout the campaign, reported that Hood intended to break the railroad above Atlanta and harass the Federal rear positions.

Governor Joseph Brown

President Jefferson Davis

Hood began by calling all reserve units from other areas. Ghoulson's and Iverson's brigades were called in to shore up a move back across the Chattahoochee River. Once again, he relied on the Texas Cavalry to lead the effort. The diary of Lt. Col. Grissom of the 9th Texas Cavalry indicates their movements to secure a line of defense for Hood's move north of the river:

September 19, 1864 - Move out on Pumpkintown Road and camp within 2m of Campbellton - Kilpatrick is there - make works for him and picket near town...

September 20, 1864 - Move at light on the Cross Anchor Road and take the Moore's Bridge and camp - 22m...

September 21, 1864 - Move at 8 a.m. (2m) and cross Chattahoochee on a pontoon at Moore's Bridge and taking up the river on the Campbellton Road camp on Dog River - 9th on picket, entire division crosses river today -rains hard...

September 22, 1864 - Relieved from picket by the 27th (Texas) and go to camp - select our own camp - saddle at II a.m. and at 1 p.m. Brigade moves 5m up Chattahoochee River and camp and just as we unsaddle and get forage in the rain have to move camp 1/4 of a mile and camp again - much sport of the abundance of Yellow Jackets...

September 23, 1864 - Brigade relieved by Ferguson's and Lewis' Brigades and move back to Phillip's Ferry and meet our train...

September 25, 1864 - Move at 7 a.m. to relieve Lewis' Brigade on Dog River and camping nearly opposite Pumpkintown put out pickets and camp...

September 26, 1864 - Move at 7 a.m. and take position further on the right - nearly opposite Campbellton - I go on picket (9th)...

September 29, 1864 - Move at 8 a.m. to Salt Springs - by 2p.m. and 9th goes on picket, picketing 5 roads taking the entire regiment...

On the 23rd of September, Hood sent Armstrong's Mississippi Cavalry across the Chattahoochee River at Davis' Ferry, two miles below Campbellton. Their mission was to scout the country in advance of the movement of the Army of Tennessee to the rear of Sherman's army at Atlanta. They made note of the fords and ferries on Sweet Water Creek all the way to Powder Springs. This would be the flank defense for Hoods line of march to Allatoona pass, the first battle after the fall of Atlanta.

Ferguson and Ross followed on the 29th, crossing at Smith's ferry and taking the pontoon train with them to Powder Springs. The crossings on the Sweet Water were effectively blockaded and Alabama and Texas Cavalry assigned to picket these strategic points. Col. William Boyles of Ferguson's Brigade was headquartered at Salt Springs behind railed barricades to guard the crossing at Sweetwater Town. He sent about 200 fellow Alabamans to Alexander's Mill to hold that position as well.

The stage was now set for the final fighting in the Atlanta Campaign.

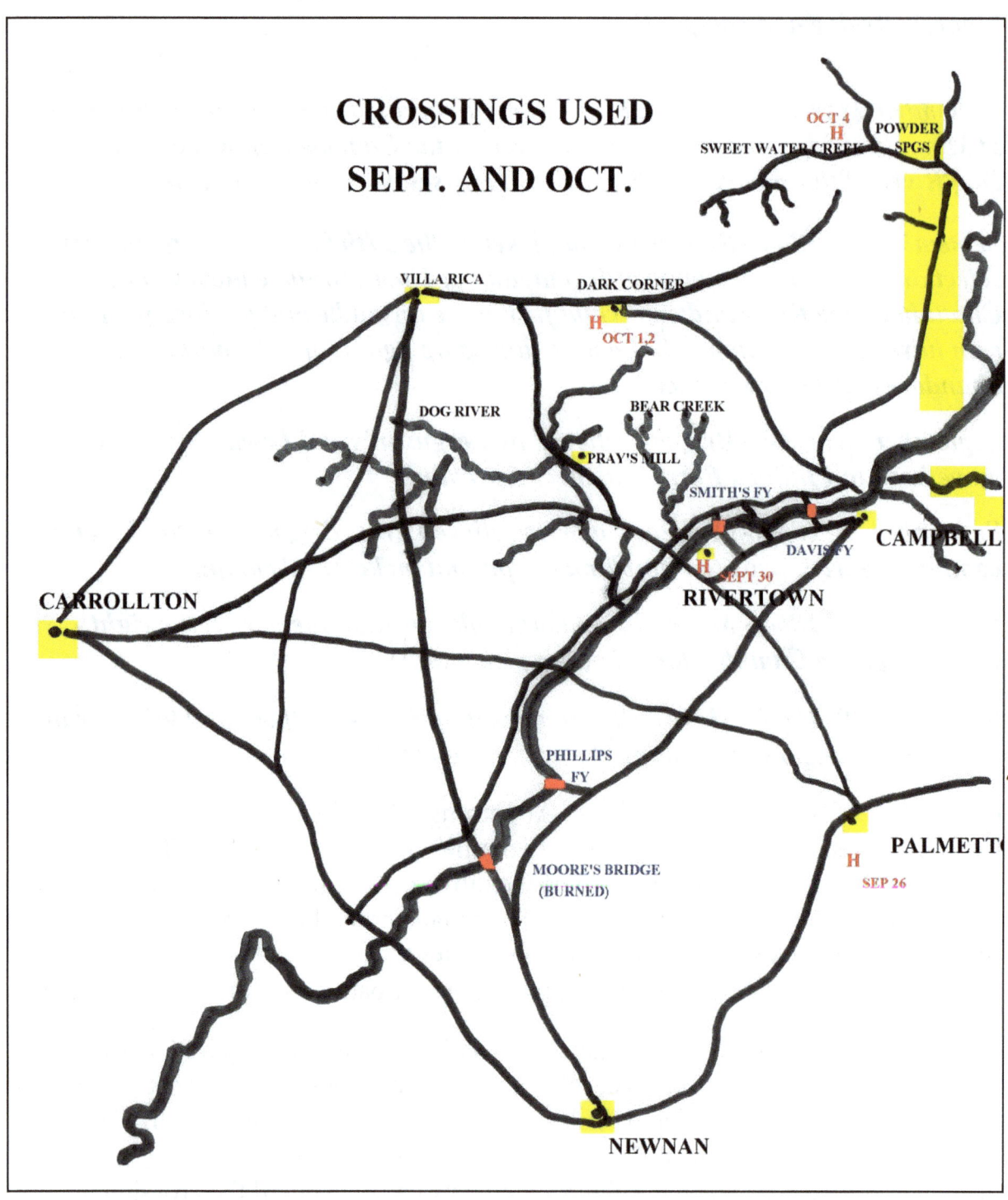

CSA artifacts from opposite Campbellton: Tower lockplate for an Enfield; portion of a Memphis Novelty Works spur; Mississippi infantry coat button; "cast I" and a rear pants buckle.

.36, .44 and .50 balls; CSA knapsack buckle and .58 Enfield.

OFFICIAL REPORTS: SEPTEMBER 1 - OCTOBER 1

Notice:
Atlanta, Ga., September 8, 1864.

To the citizens of Atlanta:
Major-Gen. Sherman instructs me to say that you must all leave Atlanta; that as many of you as want to go North can do so, and as many as want to go South can do so, and that all can take with them their movable property, servants included, if they want to go, but no force is to be used, and that he will furnish transportation for persons and property as far as Rough and Ready, from whence it is expected Gen. Hood will assist in carrying it on. Like transportation will be furnished for people and property going North, and it is required that all things contemplated by this notice will be carried into execution as soon as possible.

All persons are requested to leave their names and number in their families with the undersigned as soon as possible, that estimates may be made of the quantity of transportation required.

James M. Calhoun,
Mayor.

From Harper's: The Atlanta Railroad Depot; refugees were ordered to board trains and leave.

Executive Dept.
Milledgeville, Ga.,
September 10, 1864.

Gen. J.B. Hood,
Commanding Army of Tennessee:
General: As the militia of the State were called out for the defense of Atlanta during the campaign against it, which has terminated by the fall of the city into the hands of the enemy, and as many of these left their homes without preparation (expecting to be gone but a few weeks), who have remained in service over three months (most of the time in the trenches), justice requires that they be permitted, while the enemy are preparing for the winter campaign, to return to their homes and look for a time after important interests and prepare themselves for such service as may be required when another campaign commences against other important points in the State. I therefore, hereby, withdraw said organization from your command.

Joseph E. Brown.

September 15, 1864.

Major-Gen. Wheeler,
Commanding Cavalry:
Gen. Hood desires that you should move in this direction, in accordance with previous instructions, tearing up the railroad as you come between Chattanooga and Atlanta. He directs me to inform you that by next week the left flank of the army will rest on the Chattahoochee River, with Jackson's cavalry on the north side, where you are expected to join. When you reach the vicinity of the Etowah River communicate. Gen. Taylor has sent to Corinth 8,000 horseshoes for you.

A.P. Mason,
Asst. Adjutant-Gen.

September 15, 1864.

Brigadier-Gen. Lewis,
Commanding Cavalry Brigade, Barnesville:
Gen. Hood orders that you march your brigade to Newnan, starting on Sunday morning next, taking position there and reporting to Brigadier-Gen. Jackson, commanding cavalry division.

A.P. Mason,
Asst. Adjutant-Gen.

Palmetto, September 19, 1864 - 1:20 p.m.

Brigadier-Gen. Tyler,
West Point:
Order Gholson's cavalry brigade immediately up the west side of Chattahoochee River, opposite to Newnan, and it will therefore report to Gen. Jackson. Please come up on the first train to my Hqtrs.

J.B. Hood,
General.

William Jameson Gholson.

FED
Hqtrs. Chief of Cavalry, Dept. of the Cumberland,
Atlanta, Ga., September 18, 1864.

Brigadier-Gen. J. Kilpatrick,
Commanding Third Division Cavalry:
I am directed by the general commanding to give you the following information: G.W. Lee's battalion rebel cavalry is encamped at James Ressender's, or name similar to that, on Fayetteville Road, about six miles from Campbellton; his scouts cross the Chattahoochee at Ben Kemp's, about three miles below Campbellton. This force is very much overestimated, it is thought, at 1,200. Brown's battalion of Rice's (Ross?) brigade is camped on Fayetteville and Fairburn Road about six miles west of Fayetteville. You will, without harassing your command, endeavor to capture or rout these parties.

J.E. Jacobs,
Capt. and Asst. Adjutant-Gen.

Hqtrs. Chief of Cavalry,
Dept. of the Cumberland,
Atlanta, Ga., September 20, 1864.

Brigadier-Gen. K. Garrard,
Commanding Second Cavalry Division:
General: The general commanding directs me to inform you that it is reported the enemy has sent a pontoon train, of about 100 wagons, from Griffin towards Jonesborough, and that rebel troops are moving from Lovejoy's, in what direction is not known. The general commanding directs that you order a reconnaissance down the right bank of the Chattahoochee as far as Franklin to ascertain the movements of the enemy. General Kilpatrick has been ordered to make a reconnaissance on the left bank of the Chattahoochee for the same purpose.

J.E. Jacobs,
Captain and Asst. Adjutant-Gen.

Hqtrs. Third Cavalry Division,
Dept. of the Cumberland,
Camp Crooks (creek?),
Sept. 20, 1864 - 9:30 p.m.

Capt. J.E. Jacobs,
Asst. Adjutant-Gen., Cavalry Command:
Captain: The enemy's cavalry in considerable force occupied Campbellton at 7 p.m. this evening, and one column advanced on Sandtown Road. Another column moved from Campbellton out on the Fairburn Road, had reached Enon Church at 8 p.m. In fact all the roads from Campbellton across to Sideling approaching my front were covered at sundown this evening by the enemy's advancing cavalry. A long wagon train of the enemy went into camp sundown on the creek one-half mile beyond Campbellton. I have withdrawn my vedettes and pickets behind Camp Creek, and will make every effort to hold the stream, but my line is too long to make a successful resistance against a determined attack at any one point. If infantry was sent to hold the stream as far down as Mt. Gilead Church, I will undertake to hold the country from that point to the Chattahoochee. I send you a map of this portion of the country.

J. Kilpatrick,
Brigadier-Gen., Commanding.

Atlanta, Ga., Sept. 21, 1864 - 11:30 p.m.
(Received 2 p.m. 22d.)

Hon. E.M. Stanton,
Sec. of War:
In my dispatch today I reported that Hood was falling back. Reports just in seem to indicate that he has shifted from the Macon Road at Lovejoy's over to the West Point Road about Palmetto Station, where his men are entrenching. I will watch him, as I do not see what he designs by this movement.

W.T. Sherman,
Major-Gen.

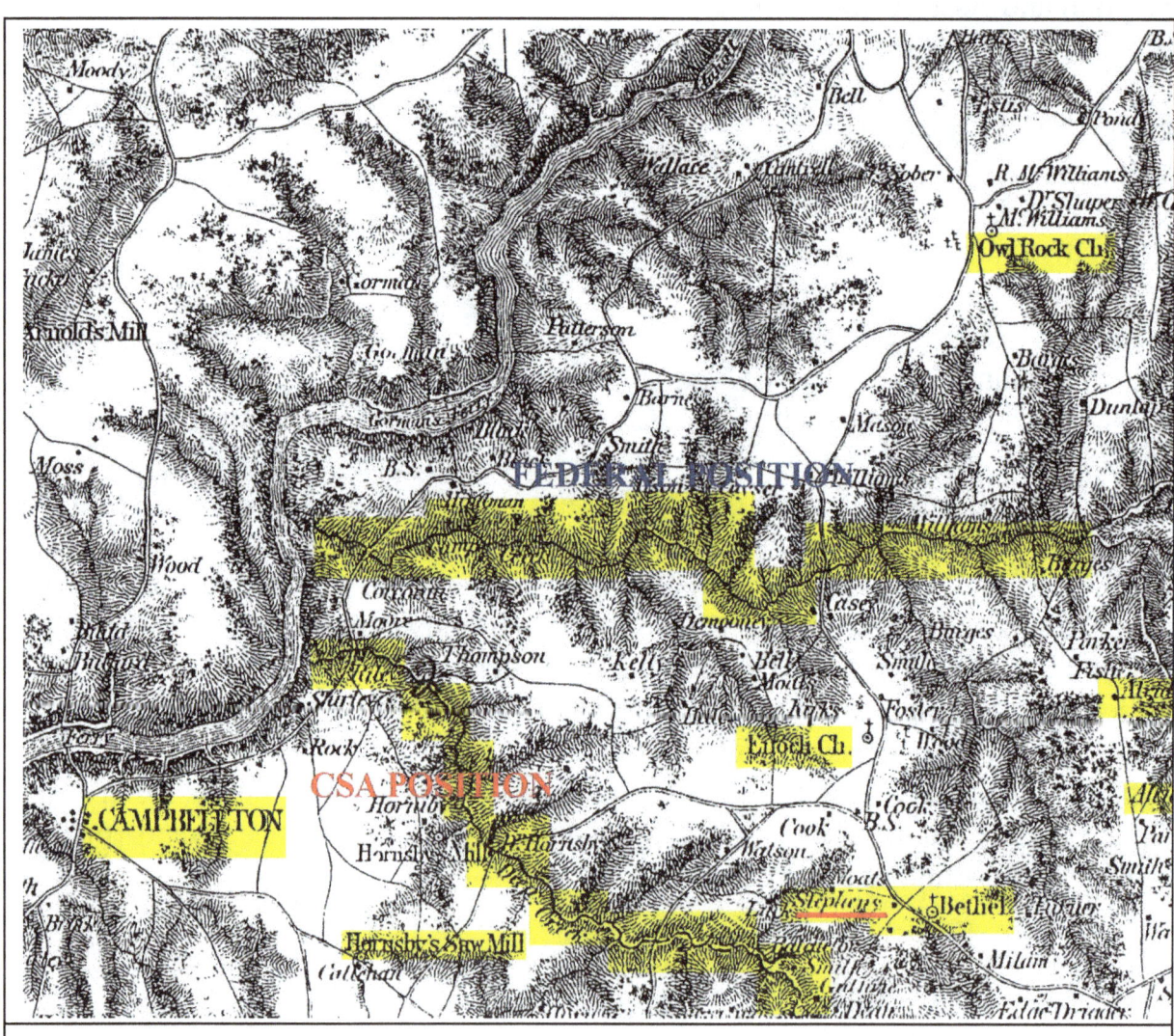

Positions of Federal and Confederate forces after the fall of Atlanta and before October 1st.

Hqtrs. Chief of Cavalry,

Dept. of the Cumberland,
Patterson's Cross-roads,
Sept. 21, 1864.

Maj. S. Hoffman,
Asst. Adj.-Gen., Hqtrs. Dept. of the Cumberland:
...Gen. K(ilpatrick) has sent scouts eight miles on the right bank of Chattahoochee. The report of pontoon bridge being there is not correct...

W.L. Elliott,
Brigadier-Gen. and Cheif of Cavalry.

Enclosure:
Sept. 21, 1864.

(Brigadier-Gen. Elliott)
Sir: My son went about three miles beyond the rebel's picket-lines. He found their first pickets near Deep Creek, at George Thompson's; that is about one mile beyond where Mr. Stevens lived. He says the rebs are thick from there as far as he went. They asked him a great many questions, and they told him that Hood was going to try to retake Atlanta. They say they will have it or die. They told him they moved up some everyday, but he could not find out where their breastworks were today. They told him Hood's entire army was along.

E.R. Aldridge.

Hqtrs. Military Division of the Mississippi,
In the Field, Atlanta, Ga., Sept. 21, 1864.

Major-Gen. O.O. Howard,
East Point:
The general wishes, if possible, that you put some persons on the track of Hood, and find out where he is going. He has been trying to get out persons from here, but does not succeed in finding any person that is worth much or reliable.

L.M. Dayton,
Aid-de-Camp.

Hqtrs. Second Cavalry Division,
Blake's Mill, Sept. 21, 1864 - 5 a.m.
(Major William H. Jennings:)
Major: ... The general thinks you had better keep the way open to Atlanta by Vining's Station, or otherwise, so that your communications will be alright. He desires also that you comply with the enclosed letter and send a reconnaissance, say, of 100 or 200 men, or more, down the right bank of the Chattahoochee (west bank) in the direction of Franklin.

Levi T. Griffin,
Capt. and Acting Asst. Adjutant-Gen.

In making the reconnaissance the general says you had better take a wagon or more, and not pack mules - that is, the party that makes the reconnaissance.

L.T.G.

On the road near Sandtown Bridge,
Sept. 22, 1864.

(Gen. Kilpatrick)
General: I left camp near Roswell yesterday morning with a detachment of the First Cavalry Brigade, Second Division, with orders to make a reconnaissance on this side of the river as far as Franklin if possible. I have 150 enlisted men and 5 officers.

C.L. Greeno,
Capt., Commanding Detachment First Cavalry Brigade.

Hqtrs. Third Cavalry Division, Dept. of the Cumberland,
Camp Crooks, Ga., Sept. 21, 1864.

Capt. J.E. Jacobs,
Asst. Adj.-Gen. to Chief of Cavalry, Dept. of the Cumberland:
Captain: Mr. Aldridge has just come in. He brings information that the enemy moved to a point two miles below Fairburn night before last, Stewart's and Hardee's corps, and are now entrenching. His first line of works cross the railroad at right angles through Wm. McClaren's garden, near the old stage stand. All last

night he was at work running his line of works toward the Chattahoochee below Campbellton. A citizen scout by name of Cook is expected in by noon; he may have additional information. He lives at Enon Church (Enoch?), and reported to me last evening that a large force of cavalry had gone into camp near his place, and that infantry encamped at Steven's Cross-roads. Col. Murray returned from a reconnaissance in direction of Fairburn. He drove in the enemy's pickets and was stopped near Sideling (Red Oak?) by a considerable force of the enemy behind barricades. Col. Sanderson reached Steven's Cross-roads and Campbellton; he confirms the report of last evening, and that the enemy moved back in direction of Fairburn and Palmetto before daylight. There may be no truth in the report about the two corps of infantry, yet all my scouts bring the same reports.

J. Kilpatrick,
Brigadier-Gen., U.S. Volunteers, Commanding Division.

Hqtrs. Third Cavalry Division,
Camp Crooks, Ga., Sept. 21, 1864.

Capt. J.E. Jacobs,
Asst. Adjutant-Gen.:
Captain: A scouting party has just returned from below Campbellton, on the opposite side (west). The enemy is not crossing. No enemy on that side. I am pushing a reconnaissance toward Fairburn and Campbellton to see what has become of his cavalry that threatened my right last evening.

J. Kilpatrick,
Brigadier-Gen., Commanding.

CSA
Palmetto, Sept. 22, 1864.

Gen. Bragg:
I shall, unless Sherman moves south, so soon as I can collect supplies, cross the Chattahoochee River, and form lines of battle near Powder Springs. This will prevent him from using the Dalton railroad and force him to drive me off or move south, when I shall fall upon his rear. I make this move, as Sherman is weaker now than he will be in the future, and I am as strong as I can expect to be...

J.B. Hood,
General.

INCIDENT AT CAMPBELLTON

The Third Texas Cavalry regiment, in their regimental history described the desolation around Campbellton:

Forty of these "jovial companionable fellows" organized themselves into a scouting squadron and set out one day to look for some excitement in the no-man's-land between the West Point railway and the Chattahoochee. Having already fought across the war ravaged countryside several times, they knew the area well. As the little band cantered up the road toward Campbellton, just south of the river, they passed almost total desolation: few farm animals survived; all the fences had long since been demolished for barricades or to fuel campfires; crops rotted in the fields; and the scattered population still remaining subsisted on corn bread and molasses.

The 3rd Texas were also the first to note the presence of Kilpatrick's Federal Cavalry, who were out on a foraging expedition:

At a farmhouse not far from Campbellton the scouts surprised two yankees in the process of dressing a plundered hog. From these captives they learned that a Federal foraging party of some sixty cavalrymen was ranging just to the south of the main road to Atlanta. Concealing themselves in the woods beside the road, the Rebels set up an ambush, intending to wipe out the foragers on their way back to the Union lines. At first everything went according to plan: presently the Yankee column approached the concealed scouts, driving a herd of milch cows ahead of them and hauling two wagonloads of plunder behind. Unfortunately, one of the Texans fired too soon and spoiled the ambush, but the Rebels fell upon the head of the column nonetheless.

Within an instant, several dozen screaming Confederate horsemen sprang into the midst of the startled foragers and began firing wildly in all directions. Private "Pem" Jarvis, of company K, lost control of his horse, which tore the pistol out of his hand as it dashed through the tangle of blackjacks and plunged into the mass of milling soldiers in the middle of the road. Jarvis repeatedly found himself the target of some Yankee's carbine, but each time one of his fellow scouts picked off his assailant before he was shot. Remarkably enough, Jarvis and his comrades emerged unscathed after killing or wounding a number of the Union soldiers before the foragers fled back toward their lines. The little band of scouts then returned to their camp with a dozen prisoners, thirty or forty captured rifles, and a wagon load of booty.

FED
Hqtrs. Dept of the Tennessee,
Sept. 22, 1864.

Major-Gen. Sherman:
A deserter reports that a bridge is laid seven miles from Newnan; that a division of cavalry has gone to Blue Mtn. to meet Wheeler...

O.O. Howard,
Major-Gen.

Enclosure:
Hqtrs. Dept. of the Tennessee.
(Sept. 23, 1864.)

Major-Gen. Sherman:
My scouts confirm the story of a bridge across the Chattahoochee about two miles below Campbellton. They found rebel cavalry pickets on the other side of the river; they crept down the river-bank till they could hear work on the bridge, but were not near enough to see it.

O.O. Howard,
Major-Gen.

Engineer button, CSA, Chapel Hill

Hqtrs. Third Cavalry Division,
Dept. of the Cumberland,
Camp Crooks, Ga., Sept. 23, 1864.

Capt. J.E. Jacobs,
Asst. Adj.-Gen. to Chief of Cavalry,
Dept. of the Cumberland:
Captain: One of Gen. Howard's scouts, Wm. Lyne, reported at dark last evening. They were opposite Campbellton, on the other side of the river. He saw troops in

and around Campbellton, heard considerable hammering, and much noise above and below the town. In the afternoon he saw a small company drilling above and to the left of the town. This confirms the report of my scouts sent you last evening. He also heard reports of two or three brigades of cavalry having crossed the river some distance below. I have small scouting parties and individual scouts in direction of Powder Springs, Carrollton, Van Wert, &c.

J. Kilpatrick,
Brigadier-Gen., Commanding.

Hqtrs. Third Cavalry Division,
Camp Crooks, Ga.,
Sept. 23, 1864 - 11 p.m.

Capt. J.E. Jacobs,
Asst. Adjutant-Gen. to Chief of Cavalry:
Captain: I have just received word from the scouting party, Second Division. Captain Greeno, commanding detachment, reports that he found the enemy's pickets about two miles this side of Davis' Ferry, six miles (sic) south of Campbellton; he drove them in, capturing two belonging to Ferguson's brigade. The prisoners report a pontoon bridge across the river at a ferry this side of Moore's Bridge, about sixteen miles south of Davis' Ferry. They also report a corps of infantry there (Gen. Stewart's command), and say that Armstrong, with his brigade, crossed the river day before yesterday for the purpose of cutting our railroad; had crowbars and picks along. Gen. Ross' brigade is also with Ferguson, with six pieces of artillery. Gen. Hood's headquarters are reported to be at some point on West Point railroad. This confirms the reports from my scouts forwarded to you last evening. Jackson's division of cavalry has certainly crossed the Chattahoochee, and all the reports go to show that the object is to strike our railroad. All quiet along my line up to this hour.

J. Kilpatrick,
Brigadier-Gen., Commanding Division.

Hqtrs. Second Brigade, Third Cavalry Division,
Owl Rock Church, Ga., Sept. 23, 1864.

Capt. L.G. Estes,

Asst. Adjutant-Gen.

Sir: At an early hour this morning I sent out two scouting parties; one of an officer and twenty-five men, who had instructions to go to Burnt Hickory, if possible, and then toward Van Wert, has just returned (3 p.m.), and reports that they met a force estimated by the officer at 150, at Sweet Water Bridge, near the old camp of this brigade at Sweet Water, which prevented the scout from crossing the creek. When first discovered, the advance, consisting of about 50 men, were seemingly endeavoring to construct a crossing where the bridge had been previously destroyed. The officers in charge of the scout did not dare, with the force mentioned in his rear, proceed on the west side of Sweet Water toward Burnt Hickory, and therefore returned. I have another scouting party out nearer to the river, which will undoubtedly strike the flank of the same party of the enemy, and gain more information as to its destination. The officer in charge of the first-named detachment learned from citizens that at Powder Springs the enemy have an encampment of about 250 men, who style themselves scouts. Shall I endeavor to send a force to Burnt Hickory? It will require (I submit with due deference) 150 or 200 men to get that far with any safety.

Thomas W. Sanderson,
Lt. Col., Cmdg. Second Brigade,
Third Division.

Endorsement:
Hqtrs. Third Cavalry Division,
Dept. of the Cumberland,
Camp Crooks, Ga.,
Sept. 23, 1864.

Respectfully forwarded for the information of the Chief of Cavalry. I cannot detach with safety to my command a sufficient force to send across the Sweet Water. The enemy in my front is strong and bold.

J. Kilpatrick,
Brigadier-Gen., Commanding.

Hqtrs. Second Brigade, Third Cavalry Division,
Camp Crooks, Ga., Sept. 23, 1864.

Capt. L.G. Estes,
Asst. Adjutant-Gen.:
Sir: The scout I mentioned in my communication of this afternoon as having been sent out down the Chattahoochee on the northwest side has returned, and reports that about one hour after the first party had left Sweet Water Bridge they arrived there, and learned that the rebel cavalry had gone back in great haste and confusion. They also learned that there was about 150 of them, and that finding a force on the northwest side of the creek they abandoned the idea of crossing, supposing (as citizens say) that the force I sent out was large. The scout just returned found a detachment of 200 men, under a captain (Greeno) of the Second Cavalry Division, at Alexander's Ford. The captain in command refused to say where he was going. Citizens all say that Ross' rebel brigade is encamped at Powder Springs.

Thomas W. Sanderson,
Lt. Col., Commanding Second Brigade.

Hqtrs. Chief of Cavalry, Dept. of the Cumberland,
Atlanta, Ga., Sept. 23, 1864.

Respectfully forwarded.
The detachment of Second Cavalry Division is probably the command sent on reconnaissance down right bank of Chattahoochee to Franklin. This communication refers to one from Col. Sanderson, herewith enclosed, submitted to the Major-Gen. commanding this evening.

W.L. Elliott,
Chief of Cavalry.

MORE GHOSTS ON SWEET WATER CREEK

In the 12 years I have spent in field work around Sweet Water Creek, I have met a number of fellow civil war buffs and local historians. They have some very strange stories to tell about the goings on there. This prompted a fellow historian to bring in a noted clairvoyant to see what might be said about the area. The lady seer was vague, but suspected ghosts of all kinds, specifically Indians drowned in the creek. A year or so later, the graves of 6 people, Indian by archeological evidence, were found near the road where Skyview Drive crosses the Sweet Water. They had apparently drowned trying to cross the creek, the wagon capsizing in high, rushing waters. Broken bones seemed to indicate that.

Several years later, a friend of mine who lives in the area was driving to work one morning, crossing on Skyview Drive from west to east. It was a foggy morning, especially near bodies of water. As he approached the bridge he spotted a figure coming out of the woods along the road on the other side of the creek. The man appeared to have on a blue raincoat wearing a kepi or forage hat. My friend said he saw him as clear as day, but when he passed over the creek and looked in the rearview mirror, he was gone.

My friend's son had a similarly hair-raising experience while camping overnight at the mouth of Sweet Water Creek. He and fellow campers were awakened in the middle of the night by the sound and specter of dozens of men on horseback, galloping at full speed, past them in the fog.

Now you may dismiss all this as second hand legends and such, but I have my own story to tell:

About ten years ago, I took the kids camping atop the hill overlooking Alexander's Mill. I spent the day with a metal detector around the ruins of the Alexander house, discovering some of the Civil War artifacts seen in this book and the kids chased up and down hills until they were completely bushed. Being a light sleeper did not prepare me for the hard ground, but I did manage to drop off.

In the middle of the night, I was awakened by a distinct **boom, boom, boom** sound, coming from the direction of the Chattahoochee River, 2 miles south and downhill from me. I heard it many times that night, but dismissed it as freight cars unloading merchandise from Fulton Industrial Park. Months later, while researching the Confederate rifle pits and trenches, on the opposite side of the river, near Sandtown, I learned that the trains had discontinued use of that particular track for several years. This left me thinking of the many cannon battles fought around Sandtown during the Atlanta Campaign.

MORE GHOSTS AND STRANGE EVENTS DOWN ON THE CHATTAHOOCHEE RIVER:

The history of a place includes the strange stories that have been passed down through the years. Stories of soldiers shot down in the middle of the road and left for the returning citizens to bury after the battle. At Campbellton, there are many vignettes of the Civil War. There are many Confederate and Federal dead buried in the local cemeteries. Their stories are not well known because they were found in or near the town after the armies moved on. The federals in the cemetery may be those killed during the McCook raid or the incident at Campbellton, involving Texas Cavalry and Kilpatrick's men. The Confederates may in fact be those killed by a single bolt of lightning, which struck a tree, discharging stacked guns in the camp beneath it, as reported but never located in the historical record.

There are stories of giant snakes, Sherman's men visiting Campbellton in 1863, during the Rome Campaign and others. But the strangest comes from a noted author and collector of Civil War relics. He told me that while metal detecting many years ago at Campbellton, near the river, he had the presence of mind to stop and take off his earphones. A noise made him turn about, where he stared face to face with an alligator, which menacingly hissed at his every move. I had heard of legends of great monsters guarding the treasures of antiquity and I guess this is our local equivalent. After all, 'gators do live in some of the ponds around here and are spotted at Sweet Water Creek Park occasionally.

In 1992, I visited a couple who lived on the road between Campbellton and Sandtown. They raised Chihuahua puppies and my kids just had to have one. That taken care of the subject somehow turned to the history of the area. They were amazed to hear of what had transpired on the road they live on, enough to comment on something they had seen many times on the river bank, not far from their own back yard. In the early morning or evening, on some days, they would see an old gentleman dressed in a grey overcoat walking down by the river. Always seen at a distance, the man was never there when approached.

Hqtrs. Military Division of the Mississippi,
In the field, Atlanta, Ga., Sept. 23, 1864.

Gen. Grant, City Point:
I do want very much a good cavalry officer to command, and have been maneuvering three months to get Mower here, but Canby has sent him up White River. My present cavalry need infantry guards and pickets, and it is hard to get them within ten miles of the front. If you think Ayres will do, I would like him. Romeyn B. Ayres, is, or was, as bad a growler as Granger. I would prefer Gregg or Wilson; still anybody with proper rank will be better than Garrard. Kilpatrick is

well enough for small scouts, but I do want a man of sense and courage to manage my cavalry, and will take anyone that you have tried.

W.T. Sherman,
Major-Gen. Commanding.

CSA
Palmetto,
Sept. 23, 1864.

Commanding Officer of Armistead's Brigade,
Opelika, Ala.:
Move with your command without delay to Phillip's Ferry, opposite Newnan, and report to Brigadier-Gen. W.H. Jackson, commanding cavalry.

J.B. Hood,
General.

FED
Hqtrs. Chief of Cavalry, Dept. of the Cumberland,
Atlanta, Ga., Sept. 24, 1864.

Gen. K. Garrard,
Second Cavalry Division:
Gen. McArthur, at Marietta, reports that Col. Roger's command, at Acworth, has been skirmishing two days with Armstrong's brigade, encamped at Villa Rica and Pumpkin Vine Creek. He also reports that there is a force at Hickory Flats, probably Hickory Level noted on map, doing damage to telegraph today. From Powder Springs return to Roswell via New Hope, Allatoona Creek, and Acworth, then to Blake's Mill.

W.L. Elliott,
Brigadier-Gen. and Chief of Cavalry,
Dept. of the Cumberland.

Hqtrs. Second Cavalry Division,
Sweet Water, Sept. 24, 1864.

Brigadier-Gen. Elliott,
Chief of Staff:
General: I have at this point met the force from Roswell. There is nothing at Campbellton. Men have been on the bank on this side and could not even see smoke. There is no bridge within twenty miles of Campbellton, but the force from my division went down some six miles below, following the river road, drove in some pickets and captured three prisoners. From these and citizens, all of whom agree, it is ascertained that Armstrong, with one brigade, has gone to the rear of us, and Ferguson and Ross were to follow, but had not yet done so. Armstrong crossed on Wednesday. There is a pontoon bridge about twenty miles of Campbellton, which has been thrown there since the cavalry crossed, at which time it was at Morris' (Moore's) Bridge, farther down the river...

K. Garrard,
Brigadier-Gen., Commanding Division.

Hqtrs. Military Division of the Mississippi,
In the field, Atlanta, Ga.,
Sept. 26, 1864 - 10 p.m.
(Received 3:15 a.m. 27th.)

Lt. Gen. U.S. Grant,
City Point:
...Hood is now on the West Point Road, twenty-four miles south of this, and draws his supplies by that road. Jeff Davis is there today, and superhuman efforts will be made to break my road. Forrest is now Lt. General and commands all the enemy's cavalry.

W.T. Sherman,
Major-Gen.

CSA
Hqtrs. Brigade,
Sept. 27, 1864 - 6 p.m.

Gen. W.H. Jackson:

General: I have just learned that Gholson's brigade is stopping below Dog River and is not at Dark Corner, as you supposed. I have had posts of my brigade near Dark Corner, but relieved them this morning, thinking Gholson's brigade would reach there this morning early. The enemy's cavalry started down in direction of Campbellton this evening, but retired as a force from Col. Boyles' brigade was sent to meet them. I send you report from Lt. Loud.

L.S. Ross,
Brigadier-Gen.

September 26, 1864.

Capt. Sykes:
Sir: By Capt. Harvey's order, I am scouting on Sweet Water, the creek our limit. There are no Federals on the south side (west) of the creek. One hundred and fifty came down to Ferguson's pickets on the 23d. We met them at the creek, and had not our courier missed his way, would have given Gen. Ferguson ample time to have entrapped them. At Captain's suggestion I enclose a map of the portion of the creek on which I am scouting. The two prominent fords on the creek, at Jones' plantation and Alexander's Mill, are one mile and two miles from the mouth of Sweet Water. The next ford is at Cooper's, which has been blockaded, but crossing very good; this is five miles from Alexander's Mill. The ford at Oldtown (Sweet Water Town) bridge is three miles from Cooper's, the two latter fords not used by the Federals opposite Gorman's Ferry, three miles from Sandtown, and one from the mouth of Sweet Water. We send a fine lot of beef cattle.

Thomas B. Loud,
Commanding Detachment
Harvey's Scouts.

FED
Hqtrs. Military Division
of the Mississippi,
Atlanta, Sept. 28, 1864.

Gen. Thomas:
I have just returned from Howard's. I think that a movement of all our cavalry not actually on picket should be made rapidly on Carrollton, to interrupt any Communication from Hood's army at Palmetto with his cavalry over about the

Tennessee. After striking Carrollton it should move boldly up toward Hood's army, and then draw back to Sandtown.

W.T. Sherman,
Major-Gen.

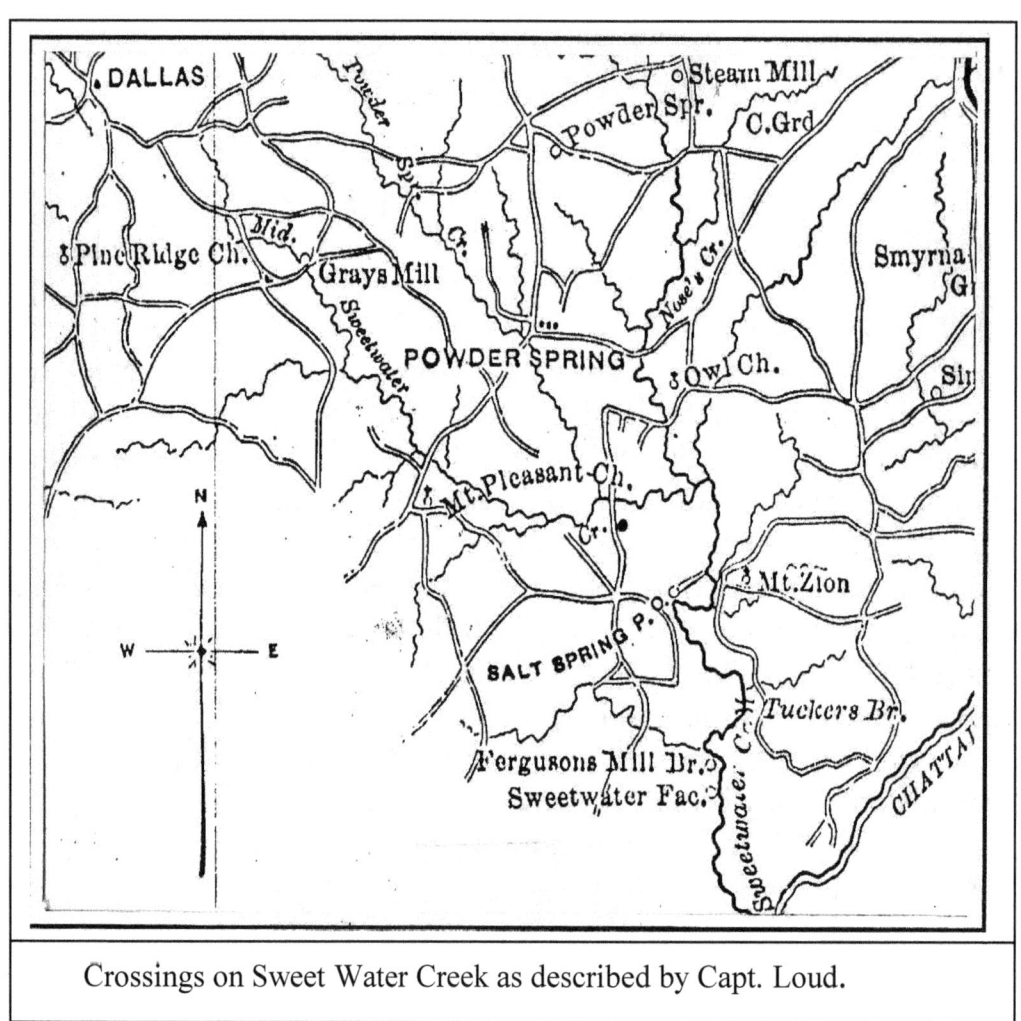
Crossings on Sweet Water Creek as described by Capt. Loud.

Atlanta, Sept. 28, 1864.

Gen. Garrard,
Commanding Second Division Cavalry:
Detail one regiment for picket at Blake's Mill and another for Roswell. Concentrate the remainder of your division, with battery, on right bank of the Chattahoochee,

near the railroad bridge or Sweet Water Town - preferably at the latter point - and be prepared for a rapid movement of five or six days...

W.L. Elliott,
Brigadier-Gen., Chief of Cavalry.

Rome, Sept. 28, 1864.

Capt. L.M. Dayton,
Aid-de-Camp:
Major Hughes, with the Ninth Illinois Mounted Infantry, arrived this morning. He struck the enemy at Van Wert; drove them through the town, capturing 5 prisoners and 12 horses. The major reports that Hardee crossed his entire corps and was moving on Blue Mtn. Armstrong's brigade passed south through Dallas Sunday morning.

Jno. M. Corse,
Brigadier-Gen., Commanding.

CSA
Sept. 28, 1864.

Brigadier-Gen. Jackson,
Commanding Cavalry:
Gen. Hood directs me to inform you that a wagon train loaded with commissary supplies will be sent this evening from Newnan, Ga., to cross the river at Phillip's Ferry, and thence to Lick Skillet (sic), where the stores will be unloaded and the train returned. He desires that you will send a regiment of cavalry to escort this train and protect the stores after they are unloaded. The escort could meet the train at whatever point you think best.

A.P. Mason,
Asst. Adjutant-Gen.

Palmetto, Sept. 29, 1864 - 8 a.m.

Lt.-Gen. Lee, Commanding Corps:

I have just written Gen. Stewart that unless some movement of the enemy in his front should prevent that he would commence to move his command to cross the river as soon as he received my note instead of waiting until 12 m. today. Gen. Hood desires that unless some movement of the enemy in your front should prevent you should mass your troops close to the river this evening, and that if Gen. Stewart's command should be out of your way that you cross as much of your command as possible, say one or two divisions. Gen. Hood thinks it would be well to send your wagon trains this morning out of your way to cross where Gen. Cheatham's command does.

A.P. Mason,
Asst. Adjutant-Gen.

Sept. 29, 1864.

Brigadier-Gen. Govan,
Commanding, &c.:
Gen. Hood desires that your brigade remain in its present position until tomorrow evening, when you will move to Moore's Bridge, on the Chattahoochee River, taking position there, with your sharpshooters on this side and your battery in position on this side of the river, or make such disposition as you think best for holding the bridge. Gen. Hood's headquarters will be at Pumpkin Town, on the other side of the river.

A.P. Mason,
Asst. Adjutant-Gen.

Gen. Daniel C. Govan

FED
Hqtrs. Military Division of the Mississippi,
In the field, Atlanta, Sept. 29, 1864.

Brigadier-Gen. Elliott,
Commanding Cavalry, Dept. of the Cumberland:

General: I am instructed by the general-in-chief to say that a man just in from Hood's (headquarters) reports Hardee's Corps moving at 5 this a.m., and he desires the cavalry to reconnoiter down toward Carrollton for obtaining information as soon as possible, but not for fighting, and to report accordingly.

L.M. Dayton,
Aide-de-Camp.

Hqtrs. Military Division of the Mississippi,
In the field, Atlanta, Ga., Sept. 29, 1864.

Brigadier-Gen. Elliott,
Chief of Cavalry, Dept. of the Cumberland:
Gen. Howard reports symptoms of Hood's crossing the Chattahoochee to the west. You may instruct Garrard to send down, say a brigade, to Kilpatrick to enable him to watch the movement, and also let him push his shoeing and be ready. Our cavalry must do more, for it is strange Forest and Wheeler should circle around us thus. We should at least make ten miles to his hundred.

W.T. Sherman,
Major-Gen.

Hqtrs. Chief of Cavalry, Dept of the Cumberland,
Atlanta, Ga., Sept. 29, 1864.

Maj-Gen. W.T. Sherman,
Commanding Military Division of the Mississippi:
I have the honor to acknowledge the receipt of your note of this day. I have ordered the brigade of Garrard's division now at the railroad bridge to Sweet Water Creek, instructing the commanding officer to receive orders from Gen. Kilpatrick and notified the latter. Gen. Kilpatrick reports that the enemy has pickets on Sweet Water and that he is watching their movements; has nothing more to confirm Gen. Howard's suspicions. This information he gave me before your note was received. Gen. Garrard assures me that he will lose no time to have his command ready. I will endeavor to do all that it is possible to do. Gen. Kilpatrick's information is not often reliable.

W.L. Elliott,

Brigadier-Gen. and Chief of Cavalry.

Cartersville, Sept. 30, 1864.

Major J.C. McCoy,
Aide-de-Camp:
One of Jackson's scouts captured here today states that Jackson was at Campbellton on Saturday, with Ross', Lewis', Armstrong's, and Ferguson's brigades, and was crossing to this side of the Chattahoochee.

E.M. McCook,
Brigadier-Gen.

Marietta, Sept. 30, 1864.

Major-Gen. Sherman:
Deserters and citizens report the following: Hood, with his army in three columns, crossed the Chattahoochee on Sunday last at Campbellton, above and below. Citizens on their line of march told them that the soldiers (rebel) said they were going to Rome. I have sent scout in that direction and will soon hear from there. All quiet here.

Gen. Kenner Garrard

J. McArthur,
Brigadier-Gen.

Rome, Sept. 30, 1864.

Major-Gen. Sherman:
The judge (Wright) is here waiting for the two gentlemen (Hill and Foster). He reports Hood's army across the Chattahoochee, a portion at Villa Rica, all moving on Blue Mtn.; their cavalry at Carrollton.

Jno. M. Corse,
Brigadier-Gen.

Hqtrs. Chief of Cavalry, Dept. of the Cumberland,
Atlanta, Ga., Sept. 30, 1864.

Captain: The following dispatch from Gen. Kilpatrick:

Hqtrs Third Cavalry Division,
Sept. 30, 1864 - 10:30 a.m.

Have had considerable skirmishing in my front this a.m. on Camp Creek; have driven the rebel cavalry back across the Sweet Water. They are now barricading the fords on that stream. Had 2 men killed and 5 wounded, and lost several horses killed and wounded. I have 100 men on the opposite side of the river watching the Sweet Water. I have very few people to guard so long a line; my pickets from Mt. Gilead Church to the left should be relieved by infantry; 150 men will be sufficient; can they not be spared?

J. Kilpatrick.

The brigade of Second Division from Roswell has probably reached the Sweet Water by this Time, although it is small.

W.L. Elliott,
Brigadier-Gen. and Chief of Cavalry,
Dept. of the Cumberland.

Capt. L.M. Dayton,
Aide-de-Camp.

2ND CAVALRY DIVISION JOINS THE FIGHT

Brig. Gen. Kenner Dudley Garrard, who had been on the left flank of the Federal army, before Atlanta, was called up to move to the right and shore up Kilpatrick's sagging defenses. Garrard's cavalry would see action near Powder Springs and later at Dallas, as Hood's troops moved north. Garrard's brigades included:

1st Brigade

Col. Robert Minty

4th Michigan Cavalry
Major Frank Mix
Capt. L. B. Eldridge
7th Pennsylvania Cavalry
Major William Jennings
4th U. S. Cavalry
Capt. James McIntyre

2nd Brigade
Col Eli Long
Col. B. B. Egglestone

1st Ohio Cavalry
Lt. Col. Thomas Patton
3rd Ohio
Col. Charles Seidel
4th Ohio Cavalry
Lt. Col. Oliver Robie

Col. Robert Minty

3rd Brigade
Col. Abram Miller

17th Indiana Mounted Inf.
Major Jacob Vail
72nd Indiana Mounted Inf.
Lt. Col. Samuel Kirkpatrick
98th Illinois Mounted Inf.
Lt. Col. Edward Kitchell
123rd Mounted Infantry
Lt. Col. Jonathon Biggs

Artillery

Chicago Board of Trade Battery
Lt. George Robinson

It was Capt. Greeno of 2nd Cavalry Division's 7th Pennsylvania unit which met Lt. Col. Sanderson's of 10th Ohio (Kilpatrick's 3rd Cavalry Division), as scouts, at

Alexander's ford on the 23rd of September, facing Col. Boyles Alabama Confederate pickets at the crossing.

As Hood got closer to the railroad after October 1st, and Kilpatrick found himself covering several miles from Camp Creek all the way to Powder Springs. He sought aid and got several of Kenner Garrard's units to bolster both Camp Creek and Sweet Water Creek fronts.The fighting at the Sweet Water Town bridge on October 1-3 included Kilpatrick's 2nd, 3rd and 5th Kentucky, the 10th Ohio, the 10th Wisconsin Battery as well as Garrard's 92nd Illinois and 4th Michigan.

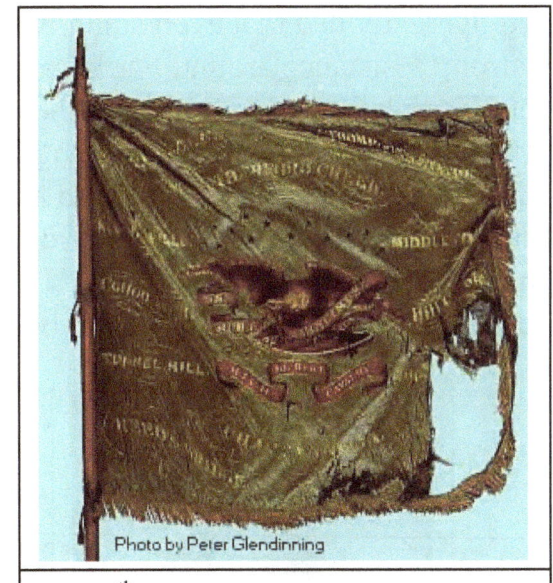

4th Michigan regimental flag

4th Ohio regimental flag.

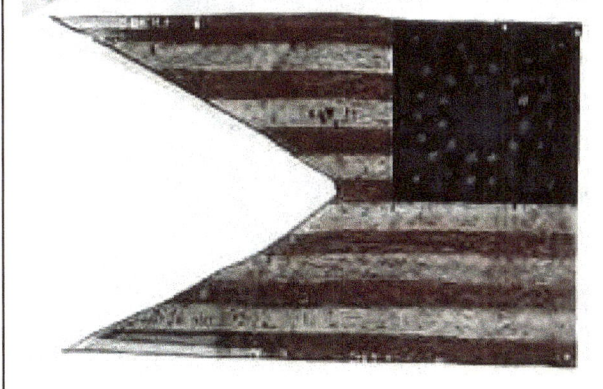

92nd Illinois Mounted Infantry guidon

98th Illinois Mounted Infantry flag

CHAPTER 7 OCTOBER 1 - NOVEMBER 11

A silence fell over the battlefields after the fall of Atlanta and for the Federals all of Hood's movements remained secretive. The majority of the Federal Army was at or near Jonesboro, with some cavalry back toward the Chattahoochee between Sandtown and Fairburn. In mid-September, restrained by a cease-fire to remove civilians from the Atlanta area, Sherman cautiously sent out scouting parties to ascertain the whereabouts of Hood and his army.

Gen. Kilpatrick quickly realized his brigade was covering a front from near Fairburn to near Powder Springs. He was so overextended that even small forces of Confederates presented a threat. He noted strong resistance around Fairburn and reports of the enemy crossing the river about Campbellton. On the 20th, Sherman sent Gen. Thomas' infantry toward Fairburn to shore up Kilpatrick's sagging line. He also sent a scouting party from 2nd Cavalry Division to make a dash to Moore's Bridge to see what was going on. When some of the scouts came to the bridge at Sweet Water Town, they found it fortified: "*....estimated by the officer at 150 ....(9-23-64).*" This was perhaps the first inkling that the Sweet Water had been blockaded by Hood's Cavalry.

Sherman then sent another scouting party to Moore's Bridge. Capt. Greeno of 1st brigade, later met up with the other scouting party:

...The scout just returned found a detachment of 200 men, under a Captain of the 2nd Cavalry Division, at Alexander's Ford. The Captain in command refused to say where he was going...(9-23-64).

Captain Loud of Harvey's Confederate Scouts also showed up and later reported:

Captain Greeno, 7th Pa. Cav.

...One hundred and fifty came down to Ferguson's pickets on the 23rd. We met them at the creek, and had not our courier missed his way, would have given General Ferguson ample time to have entrapped them...(9-23-64).

152

As news of other Confederate cavalry at Powder Springs arrived, Gen. Sherman contemplated a mad dash by all cavalry to intercede between Hood and his cavalry. He intended to head straight for Carrollton to meet Hood head on. To achieve this he sent Kilpatrick farther north to Powder Springs and summoned Garrard to move west to the Sweet Water Town bridge. He also noted the intention of Hood, whose army was visited by Jefferson Davis on the 26th, to cross the Chattahoochee in force to cut the railroad north of Marietta.

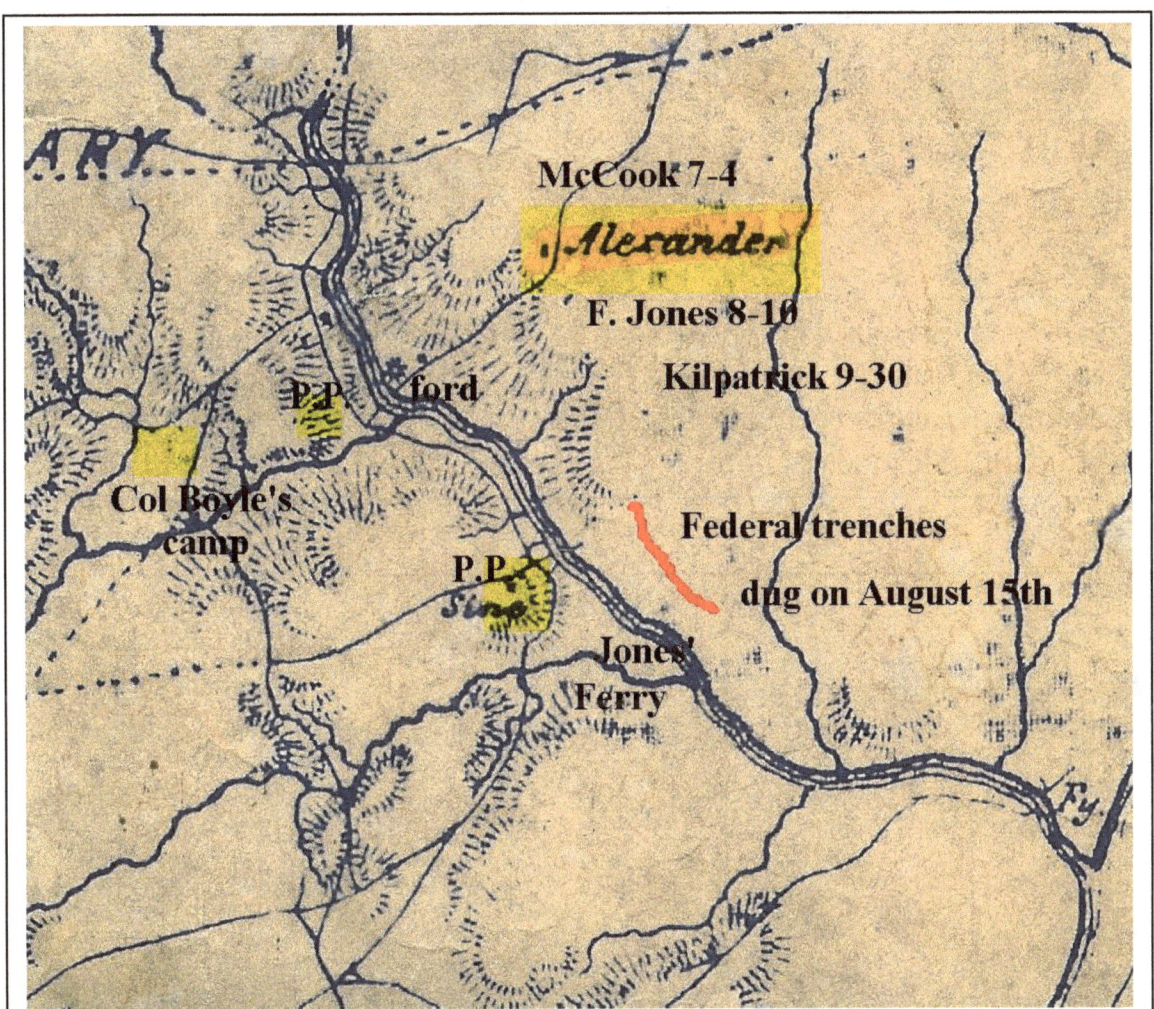

Alexander's Mill and Ford, scene of battle between Kilpatrick's and Col. Boyles' cavalry on September 30th and former campsite of both McCook's and Fielder Jones' brigades. Here Col Sanderson and Captain Greeno's scouts met on the 23rd of September and were nearly captured by Col. Boyles' men. Fired bullets were found on either side of the creek at both Alexander's Ford and the Jones' Ferry crossing just below.

The Alexander House; dropped and fired bullets found around the house and at the picket posts on the hills overlooking Alexander's Ford.

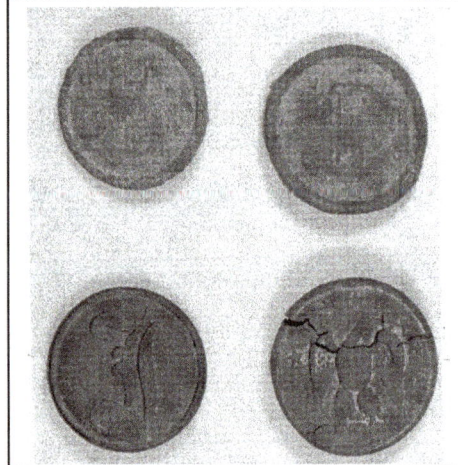

Confederate buttons from the camp opposite Alexander's Mill: tin back block, Pewter "I", Script "I" and 11 star eagle button.

Two bayonets: upper is a Ga. State Troop type from the mouth of Sweet Water Creek, the 2nd is a short musket carbine type, from Col. Boyles' camp opposite Alexander's Mill.

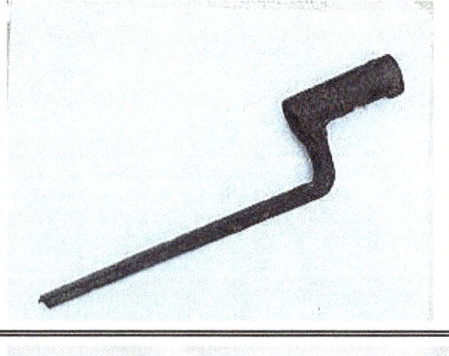

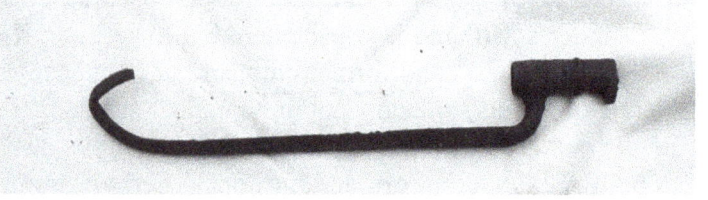

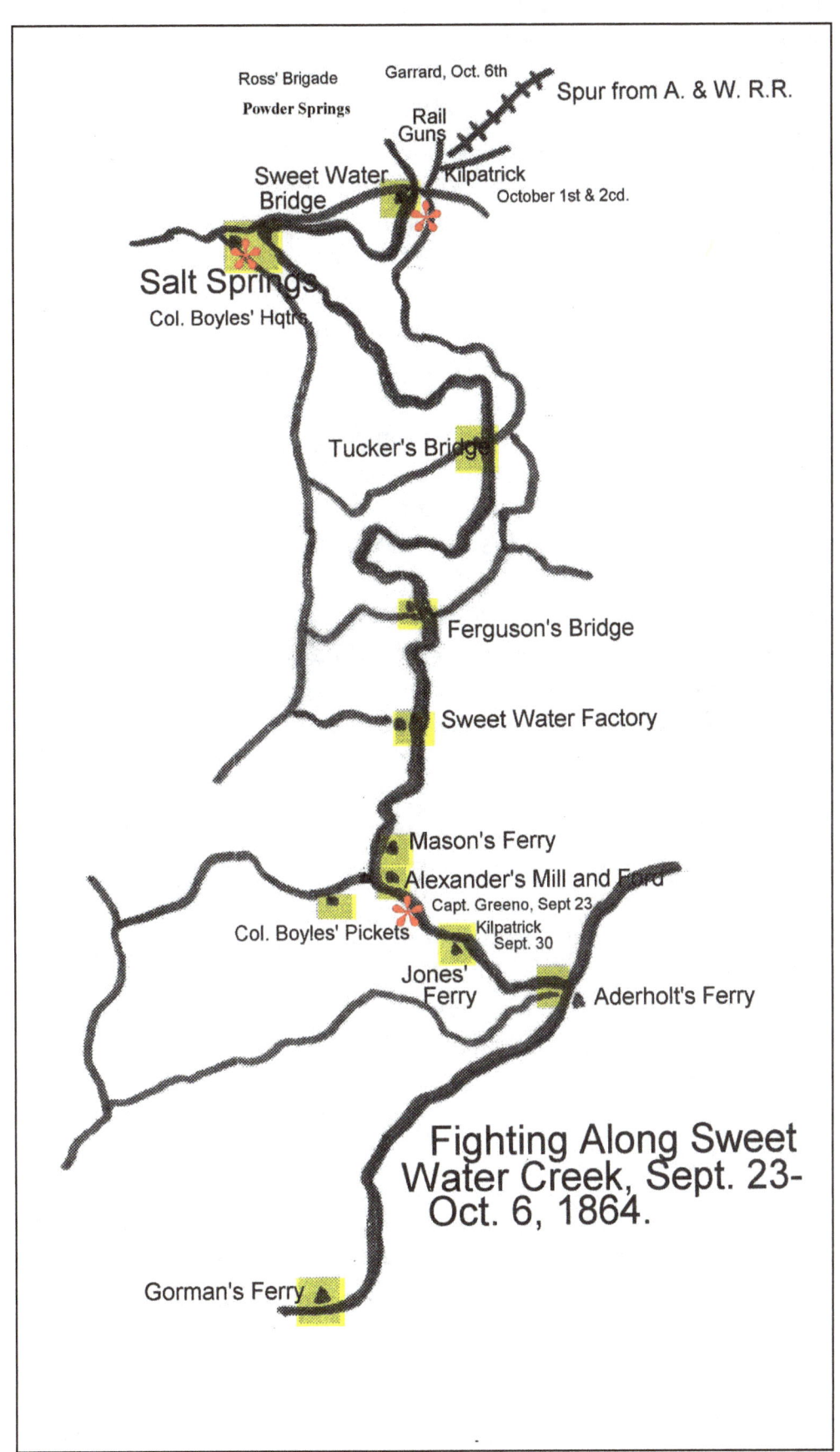

On September 30th, Kilpatrick began to feel Confederate pressure to hold the Sweet Water Creek flank:

Have had considerable skirmishing in my front this a.m. on Camp Creek; have driven the rebel cavalry back across the Sweet Water. They are now barricading the fords on that stream. Had 2 men killed and 5 wounded, and lost several horses killed and wounded. I have 100 men on the opposite side of the river watching the Sweet Water.

On October 1st, as Hood's Army started crossing the River at Pumpkintown, Kilpatrick began his attempt to cross the Sweet Water at Sweet Water Town bridge. Col. Boyles of Ferguson's Alabama Cavalry Brigade reported a railroad line had been constructed down to his position on the creek and heavy rail guns brought to bear on Salt Springs and that he heard drum and band music on the Sandtown - Marietta Road and skirmishing below the bridge at a ford. The next day he found himself in a fight for his life:

Captain (Sykes): Enemy made a bridge on Sweet Water above this point last night, and under cover of artillery have crossed a heavy cavalry force. The length of my line and the absence of Col. Inge's regiment neccessitates reinforcements. I have only 600 fighting men.

Kilpatrick, having tried earlier to secure a bridgehead was "*...driven back after a severe skirmish...(10-1-64)*" but managed to cross, drive Col. Boyles back 1.5 miles and finish building the bridge. Boyles reported the movement: "*....leaves my pickets on the lower Sweet Water exposed, and I have concentrated them at Alexander's Mill. I don't think I can hold my position if attacked. I can only bring into a fight about 400 men in front...(10-2-64.)*" Meanwhile, Gen. Ross, at Powder Springs feared that Infantry moving on the Sandtown - Marietta Road could cross at Sweet Water Town Bridge and, heading down the Atlanta - Villa Rica Road, would be closer to Hood's infantry than he was. He proposed to relieve Col. Boyles to keep Federal cavalry from getting between the infantry and the cavalry.

As the Confederate infantry moved north, Sherman ordered his entire army to set out for Marietta. On the 4th, Hood's infantry were beaten back from Allatoona, Gen. Corse reinforcing from Rome, Ga. Sherman then ordered Kilpatrick to make a dash for Carrollton to chase Hood's forces westward:

Colonel (Clark): I have forced two brigades of Jackson's Cavalry Division beyond this point (Flint Hill Church), and now hold the bridge over the right branch of Sweet Water (Gothard's) and the Dallas - Campbellton Road and within three miles of the Dallas -Villa Rica Road. Rebel Cavalry have all left the lower Sweet Water and country south of this point and have gathered in about Dallas, covering the movements of Hood's army, which is not marching on any of the roads south of Dallas...(10-7-64).

Having been unsuccessful at Allatoona, Hood began his retreat into Tennessee, to fight again at Nashville and Franklin and to disband and go back to Texas, while others regrouped in South Carolina, with Gen. Johnston, only to surrender in North Carolina. On November 11, Atlanta was ordered burned and Sherman, leaving a garrison behind, would begin his march to the sea. Kilpatrick made his final report to him, noting:

Hood at Corinth; 1500 cavalry and some infantry at Opelika, 3 brigades of cavalry at Carrollton, 5 regiments at Villa Rica and a small force at West Point and Newnan.

Company D, 25th Illinois remained at Salt Springs after the war. Other camps were at Campbellton, off Mann Road, near Dark Corner and Kentucky Federals were still being snatched and hung, near Sandtown, well after the war was over. The people of Campbell, later Douglas County, had to put up with the Pony Homestead, The Freedman's Bureau and Federal Troops until 1876, when Reconstruction ended. Visiting Atlanta in the early 1960s, as a teen, I was witness to some of the earliest signs that the South might finally recover from the Civil War.

The Destruction of Atlanta before the march to the sea, from Harper's Weekly.

OFFICIAL REPORTS SEPT. 30 - NOVEMBER 11

Dark Corner,
Sept. 30, 1864.

Brigadier-Gen. Govan,
Commanding, and &c.:
Gen. Hood desires that you will give Brigadier-Gen. Iverson any aid you can in resisting any cavalry expedition against the West Point railroad, but not to allow yourself to be cut off from Moore's Bridge, as you must cross the Chattahoochee there, whenever you are ordered to join the main army.

A.P. Mason'
Asst. Adjutant-Gen.

Dark Corner,
Sept. 30, 1864.

Brigadier-Gen. Iverson;
Commanding Cavalry:
Gen. Hood desires that you should report daily in future, whether anything important transpires with you or not, he desires you to put on a line of couriers from your headquarters to Moore's Bridge, where we will have a station, or near there, as I am having a line put on to Newnan. Brigadier-Gen. Govan has been directed while he remains at Moore's Bridge to cooperate with you in resisting any cavalry movement against the West Point railroad.

A.P. Mason,
Asst. Adjutant-Gen.

Gen. Alfred Iverson

Dark Corner,
October 1, 1864.

Brigadier-Gen. Iverson,
Commanding Cavalry:
Gen. Hood directs me to inform you that he has positive information that Garrard's cavalry command has gone up the railroad and across the Etowah and that Kilpatrick's division is in your front. The Gen. desires you to hold yourself in readiness to meet Kilpatrick should he advance against you. Call upon Gen. Govan should you need assistance. Gen. H. expects you to give him prompt and reliable information of all movements.

A.P. Mason,
Asst. Adjutant-Gen.

Dark Corner,
October 1, 1864.

Brigadier-Gen. Iverson,
Commanding Cavalry,
Right Wing:
Gen. Hood desires me to say that he thinks you had better bring Lewis' brigade farther to your left - that is, nearer to the West Point railroad, unless you have some information of the enemy's movements, which makes the present position of that command neccessary. Our information here is that Kilpatrick is on this side of the Chattahoochee and Garrard's command has gone up the Chattanooga railroad. Should the enemy leave Atlanta to attack this army you must endeavor to destroy all stores the enemy may leave there.

A.P. Mason,
Asst. Adjutant-Gen.

HOOD'S ARMY CROSSES THE RIVER AT PUMPKINTOWN:

On October 1st, the wagon train for the Army of Tennessee crossed at Moore's Bridge, while the infantry crossed at Phillips Ferry:

At noon the command started, crossing the Chattahoochee that evening on a pontoon bridge at the Pumpkintown, or Phillip's Ferry and going into camp after a march of 8 miles. (D. P.Smith, Co. K, 1st Alabama Infantry.)

The 3rd made ready for the move in the early morning chill and later in the day crossed the river on a pontoon bridge at Pumpkintown, near Cross Anchor, Ga. ...(H. G. Howell, 3rd Mississippi Infantry.)

In all, nearly 30,000 infantry crossed that day. The weather included two weeks of constant rain, choking the line of march in mud. A private in Co. G. 2nd Ga., Alphonso Jackson, described the march as tiresome trudging through mud that sucked the boots off one's feet; that it took several hours to go a mile and that troops were so exhausted that when they fell out on the sides of the road, fires from the previous marchers were still lit for them to use.

In the ***History of the 25th Alabama Infantry,*** the author remembers one of the lighter moments of the march north:

In a few days the army took up the line of march back toward Tennessee. I remember we crossed Chattahochee River at a place called Pumpkin Town and soon after the crossing, our Brigade was marched out of the main road and went some distance through the woods and finally up a long bushy hollow and were ordered to stack arms and rest (I suppose General Hood was endeavoring to conceal from the enemy as far as possible the movements of his army).

I remember just as the men had been halted and stacked their guns and began to scatter about in the woods, our regiment was at the head of the column and the entire line. I suppose the whole line was nearly half mile long. Some of our regiment had strolled off in the woods a short distance above the head of the column and had aroused a wild deer from his slumber and he jumped up and in his confusion ran down the entire line of soldiers, knocking down several men as he went and finally made his escape. And such a yell as went up from the men while the deer was running among them I had never heard during the war.

FED
Atlanta, Oct. 1, 1864 - 1p.m.
(Received 7 p.m.)

Lt.-Gen. Grant, City Point:
Hood is evidently on the west side of the Chattahoochee below Sweet Water. If he tries to get on my (rail) road this side of the Etowah I shall attack him, but if he goes over to the Selma and Talladega Road why would it not do for me to leave

Tennessee to the force which Thomas has and the reserves soon to come to Nashville, and for me to destroy Atlanta, and then march across Georgia to Savannah of Charleston, breaking roads and doing irreparable damage? We cannot remain on the defensive.

W.T. Sherman,
Major-Gen.

Atlanta, Ga.,

Oct. 1, 1864 - 1 p.m.

Gen. G.H. Thomas,
Chattanooga:
Hood has evidently crossed the Chattahoochee to the west, but has not gone to Blue Mtn. Kilpatrick on the Sweet Water, reports he could hear drums at reveille. There is too much ostentation in this move of Hood's and he may attempt to swing his cavalry on our road. I have ordered Gen. Garrard over to Powder Springs. I will watch him close. Make as quick work with Forrest as you can, and get back to cooperate with me.

W.T. Sherman,
Major-Gen.

Hqtrs. Dept. of the Tennessee,
Oct. 1, 1864.

Major-Gen. Sherman:
Your dispatch received. I like the plan. I wish we had more forage on hand. The enemy having burned bridges across the Sweet Water indicates a wider sweep. I am yet loath to believe that Hood will throw his entire army across the Chattahoochee.

O.O. Howard,
Major-Gen.

Hqtrs. Military Division of the Mississippi,

Oct. 1, 1864.

Gen. Kilpatrick, Sweet Water:
I am anxious that hood should stretch over to Blue Mtn., but want to know it as soon as possible. If his infantry passes Carrollton he will go across, but if he marchs up toward Dallas he means our railroad about the Etowah Bridge or Acworth. All I want the cavalry to do is to develop Hood's design. I don't care about picket-lines, but keep cavalry in hand and motion, and watch, of course, Sweet Water Bridge, Powder Springs, and Dallas.

W.T. Sherman,
Major-Gen.

Hqtrs. Third Cavalry Division, Dept. of the Cumberland,
Sweet Water Creek, Ga., Oct. 1, 1864 - 7:30 p.m.

Brigadier-Gen. Elliott,
Chief of Cavalry:
General: All the bridges are burned on the Sweet Water and Noye's (Nose's) Creek. The Sweet Water and Noye's Creek is the enemy's line of picket; neither of these streams can be forded at present. I forced the enemy back, swam the creek at Sweet Water Town or bridge, at 1 p.m. today, but was driven back after a severe skirmish. At 4 p.m., under cover of my artillery, I made another attempt and was successful. Have about completed a bridge; it will be finished before morning, when I will push forward my reconnaissance. I hold the Sweet Water and Noye's Creek from Chattahoochee to a point near the crossing of the Powder Springs and Marietta road... I have sent scouts in every direction toward the railroad and railroad bridge, and I can learn nothing of the First Brigade, Second Division. A large train of wagons parked last evening on Sweet Water (a branch of Sweet Water) three miles from Powder Springs; scouts just report heavy rebel picket-post this side Noye's Creek on road to Marietta. I fully realize the importance of gaining reliable information, and will make every effort to see the rebel infantry tomorrow.

J. Kilpatrick,
Brigadier-Gen., Commanding.

CSA
Hqtrs. Ferguson's Brigade,
Salt Springs, Oct. 1, 1864 - 4:30 p.m.

Capt. E.T. Sykes,
Asst. Adjutant-Gen.:
Captain: The enemy has constructed railroad on the other side of the Sweet Water and has a battery in position. His pickets extend up the river, and a regiment is stationed near the crossing in front. A little skirmishing is going on at the ford immediately below. Drums and bands of music are distinctly heard, and from the direction and volume of the sound are supposed to be along the Sandtown and Marietta Road. Have received no recent report from the pickets below. The cavalry in my front could readily be cut off by a force moving from Powder Springs, unless there is some movement of the Yankee infantry to prevent.

W. Boyles,
Col., Commanding.

Hqtrs. Brigade,
Oct. 2, 1864.
Capt. E.T. Sykes,
Asst. Adjutant-Gen.:
Captain: Enemy made a bridge on Sweet Water above this point last night, and under cover of artillery have crossed a heavy cavalry force. The length of my line and the absence of Col. Inge's regiment necessitates reinforcements. I have only about 600 fighting men.

W. Boyles,
Col., Commanding.

Hqtrs. Ferguson's Brigade,
One mile west Salt Springs,
on Villa Rica Road,
Oct. 2, 1864 - 10:15 a.m.

Capt. E.T. Sykes,
Asst. Adjutant-Gen.:
Captain: The enemy, under cover of artillery and dismounted cavalry, threw a bridge over Sweet Water last night, crossed this morning, and after moving his force, cavalry as far as known, moved upon me and drove me back to this point,

flanking on both sides. This movement leaves my pickets on the lower Sweet Water exposed, and I have concentrated them at Alexander's Mill. I do not think I can hold my position if attacked. I can only bring into a fight about 400 men in front.

W. Boyles,
Col., Commanding.

Hqtrs. Division,
Oct. 2, 1864 - 10:50 a.m.
Gen. W.H. Jackson:
General: I sent a force to strike the railroad above Kennesaw Mtn. last night. Lt. Sykes, of my staff, accompanied the expedition. He informs me that there is no enemy above the Villa Rica and Marietta road, excepting the guards on the railroad. They found some infantry watching the railroad. There is a force in my front on the Powder Springs and Marietta Road and they seem disposed to try to gain possession of the bridge. From Lt. Martin I learn your plans in reference to my movements, and I have thought it not improper to suggest that as there is no enemy above me, a small force could picket toward Lost Mtn. and the balance of Armstrong's brigade take my place here and I move at once to hold the creek in Col. Boyles' front. I think there can be no doubt of the presence of Federal infantry on the creek below Col. Boyles. If they force him back and effect a crossing with cavalry and infantry, which I am inclined to believe they will attempt this morning, I would have to move by the bridge at your headquarters to cross Sweet Water and thence down to Salt Springs. It is about nine miles from this place to the latter by that bridge, and after the enemy crossed at Salt Springs or below, they would be much nearer the road the infantry marched than I, and of course much time would be consumed in preparing to move and bringing information from Col. Boyles to me. Would it not be better for me to move a part, if not all, of my division down there as soon as Gen. Armstrong can relieve me here with one of his brigades, and thus be in position to drive the enemy back should he attempt to cross?

L.S. Ross,
Brigadier-Gen.

One-Quarter Mile from Salt Springs,
On Villa Rica Road,
Oct. 2, 1864 - 12:30 p.m.

Col. Boyles was convinced rail guns such as this one were pounding Salt Springs.

Capt. E.T. Sykes,
Asst. Adjutant-Gen.:
Captain: Enemy in position at Salt Springs. Skirmishers about three-quarters of a mile in advance of their position. They have reversed the rail-works constructed by Gen. Ross and from which they drove Col. Boyles this morning. The enemy evince no disposition to advance at present - supposed to be crossing their main force over the creek. Drums can be distinctly heard from here in direction of Sandtown Road and about opposite Salt Springs. Scouts report a column moving on the road from Sweet Water Town to Powder Springs. Could not ascertain whether it was infantry or cavalry - heard wagons, and &c. Scouts just in from the railroad near Vining's Station report no infantry moving from Marietta or Atlanta except by the railroad. Four trains went up from Atlanta on night before last heavily laden with troops.

J.C. Jones, Jr.,
Aide-de-Camp

Hqtrs. Division,
Oct. 2, 1864 - 10 o'clock.

Gen. W.H. Jackson:
Gen.: I forward the following report just received:

Brigadier-Gen. Jackson,
Commanding, &c.:
General: The enemy's drums and bugles are distinctly heard this morning (9 a.m.) opposite and near to the burnt bridge on Sweet Water. The creeks are now very high, not fordable in this vicinity anywhere. The scouts I sent in the direction of the railroad yesterday have not yet returned. Occasional guns are heard in Col. Boyles' front. The enemy seems to be rather quiet this morning.

Hill Taylor,
Commanding Scouts.

L.S. Ross, Brigadier-Gen, Commanding.

P.S. - The enemy have just appeared at the bridge on Marietta and Powder Springs Road guarded by Col. Lowry's command.

L.S. Ross,
Brigadier-Gen.

Texas button like this found near Alexander's Mill on Sweet Water.

FED
Hqtrs. Military Division of the Mississippi,
In the field, Atlanta, Ga., Oct. 2, 1864.

Gen. Jeff. C. Davis: ...I think Hood has crossed the Chattahoochee with two corps to attack our road, and has left one corps on this side, near Campbellton. We should interpose.

W.T. Sherman,
Major-Gen., Commanding.

Hqtrs. Third Div. Cav., Dept. of the Cumberland,
Sweet Water Town, Oct. 2, 1864 - 7 a.m.

Brigadier-Gen. Elliott:
General: Gen. Sherman's instructions have been received. Major Jennings has arrived. I am pushing a reconnaissance toward Powder Springs and Dalton and Villa Rica. The creek is very high; cannot be forded. My bridge, I think, will stand.

J. Kilpatrick,
Brigadier-Gen., Commanding Cavalry Division.

Hqtrs. Military Division of the Mississippi,
In the field, Atlanta, Ga., Oct. 2, 1864.

Major-Gen. Howard,
Commanding Army of the Tennessee:
There is a flood in the Chattahoochee, which has damaged our railroad bridge, and will, of course, carry away any of Hood's bridges. I want that reconnaissance pushed out boldly. As soon as it reaches Fairburn let me know, as I may push it on to the rear of their bridge. All the valuable part of the enemy's cavalry is over beyond Sweet Water, and we can do them damage on this side now...

W.T. Sherman,
Major-Gen., Commanding.

Hqtrs. Dept. of the Tennessee,
Oct. 2, 1864.

Major-Gen. Sherman:
Your dispatch received. I have sent word to Gen. Ransom to report to me as soon as he arrives at Fairburn, and not to hasten his march back unless compelled to.

O.O. Howard,
Major-Gen.

Hqtrs. Military Division of the Mississippi,
In the field, Atlanta, Ga., Oct. 2, 1864.

Gen. Howard:
Let Ransom come in slowly, and if the enemy approach sally out and attack him fiercely. Gen. Davis will be in close support. I will throw Gen. Stanley across the Chattahoochee and be prepared to put our whole force in motion to interpose between Hood who may attempt to mash our road about Marietta and his bridges at Campbellton. Be prepared to send in all your troops to Atlanta, and to follow Gen. Stanley. I would attack this corps in position but presume it is strongly entrenched.

W.T. Sherman,
Major-Gen., Commanding.

Rome, Oct 2, 1864.

Major-Gen. Sherman:
There are one or two regiments of Texas cavalry living in and about Burnt Hickory and Dallas that commit the mischief done our communications. If you will send, permit me to suggest, to Dallas, via Villa Rica, I will, with a less number, drive them down, and the two commands can kill or capture the greater portion of them. If this meets with your approval please let me know at once. I propose burning Cedartown, Van Wert, and Buchanan for atrocities committed by gangs of thieves having their rendezvous at those places.

Jno. M. Corse,
Brigadier-Gen.

Hqtrs. Military Division of the Mississippi,
In the field, Atlanta, Ga., Oct. 3, 1864.

Gen. Corse,
Rome:
Hood is meditating some plan on a large scale. One corps is entrenched below Campbellton, and two corps are across below Sweet Water, about Powder Springs. I send Gens. Stanley and Davis over today, and may follow tomorrow myself with a heavy force. I am willing he should go to Blue Mtn., or to strike our road at Acworth or Cassville.

W.T. Sherman,

Major-Gen., Commanding.

CSA
Carley's House, October 5, 1864 - 10 a.m.

Brigadier-Gen. Iverson,
Commanding Cavalry:
Gen. Hood directs me to say that he has information that all Sherman's cavalry have moved to Marietta, and that the remainder of his army is moving in that direction. He directs you, therefore, that the regiment of Ferguson's brigade that is now with your command shall return at once to its own brigade at Salt Springs, and that you move Morgan's brigade at once to this side of the Chattahoochee River, to take a line from Salt Springs to Campbellton, reporting direct for orders to Gen. Jackson, by letter, as soon as he is in position. Jackson's headquarters will be near Gen. Hood's, which are at Carley's house, on the lower Dallas Road, five miles west of Lost Mtn. You must also extend your lines to your left, so as to be in communication with Gen. Morgan, at Campbellton, on the Chattahoochee River. Gen. Morgan will move at once and get into position with as little delay as possible.

A.P. Mason,
Asst. Adjutant-Gen.

Dallas, October 6, 1864 - 7 p.m.

Brigadier-Gen. Iverson,
Commanding Cavalry:
Gen. Hood directs that should Morgan's brigade not have crossed the Chattahoochee River before the pontoon bridge at Moore's is taken up that he must swim the animals and cross the men, saddles, &c., in the ferry-boat, and get over with all possible dispatch, and instead of taking position from Salt Springs to Campbellton, as previously ordered, he will move his command to Villa Rica, reporting to Brigadier-Gen. Jackson by letter at this point.

A.P. Mason,
Asst. Adjutant-Gen.

FED
Hqtrs. Military Division of the Mississippi,
In the field, Kennesaw, October 6, 1864.
(Received 5:30 a.m. 7th.)

Gen. Howard:
Order Kilpatrick if he can cross Sweet Water to dash at Powder Springs and then turn toward any or all roads leading south from Dallas. Hood is about New Hope covering a party of cavalry sent to cross the Etowah and to act against our roads there. I have intelligence from Allatoona. All well there, but Gen. Corse was wounded in the face, losing a cheek bone and an ear. I want you to impress on Kilpatrick the importance of operating rapidly and boldly against the roads by which Hood can alone move south; not to attack infantry in position but to hang about them as their cavalry does about us, and to pick up enough prisoners to make up for our losses. He should not carry a gun or wheel with him, but move and act as pure cavalry. You may at the same time move out toward Dallas a division light, without wagons or artillery, to threaten Hood and act in concert with the cavalry. Hood's precipitate movement back shows he doesn't propose to fight us on fair terms, and he knows we will not follow him far, and therefore let this infantry, with the cavalry, seem to seek a position to act against him as he retreats. Keep

The Battle of Allatoona, from Harper's Weekly.

your artillery and wagons well parked and the main force well in hand near their present positions till roads improve or until new developments are made. I will go to the top of Kennesaw tomorrow to watch. I have sent orders similar to these to all the army commanders. Gen. Garrard will threaten the roads between Hood and Burnt Hickory.

W.T. Sherman,
Major-Gen., Commanding.

Hqtrs. Military Division of the Mississippi,
In the field, Kenesaw, Oct. 7, 1864.

Gen. Elliott:
I have your communication of today and will answer at length at a more leisure time. Our cavalry is wanting in enterprise. I am fully conscious of the many difficulties which they encounter in so wooded a country and such blind roads, but 'tis useless to discuss these now. I want to prevent Hood from crossing the Allatoona range, toward the Etowah Bridge, and also to keep the infantry force employed in repairing the damage already done to our road. I wish you, therefore, to keep Garrard's division and Kilpatrick employed in harassing the enemy's rear, picking off parties and also striking whenever he offers an opportunity. His road must be equally bad as ours, and will occasion delay and straggling of which our cavalry must take advantage. I don't care of pursuing much below Dallas, but I do want to know that Hood's main army has passed below Dallas toward Carrollton. If our cavalry will make bold and handsome dashes I promise to make full and public acknowledgement of their services.

W.T. Sherman,
Major-Gen., Commanding.

Hqtrs. Third Cavalry Division,
Dept. of the Cumberland,
On Right Branch Sweet Water,
Near Flint Church, Oct. 7, 1864 - 8 p.m.

Col. W.T. Clark,
Asst. Adjutant-Gen.

Colonel: I have forced two brigades of Jackson's cavalry division beyond this point, and now hold the bridge over the right branch of Sweet Water and the Dallas and Campbellton Road and within three miles of the Dallas and Villa Rica Road. Rebel cavalry have all left the lower Sweet Water and country south of this point and have gathered in about Dallas, covering the movements of Hood's army, which is not marching on any of the roads south of Dallas...

J. Kilpatrick,
Brigadier-Gen.

Hqtrs. Dept. and Army of the Tennessee,
Oct. 8, 1864 - 1 a.m.

General: Gen. Kilpatrick has received my order to return, and will start back at 3 a.m. A citizen (lady) says that she crossed Hood's bridge day before yesterday, and that she saw his cavalry afterward set it on fire. I do not regard this as reliable information, but it may be true.

O.O. Howard,
Major-Gen.

Hqtrs. Second Cavalry Division,
New Hope, Oct 9, 1864.
(Received 4 p.m.)

Brigadier-Gen. Elliott,
Chief of Cavalry, Dept. of the Cumberland:
General: ...The enemy are in great fear, from what I learn, that Sherman will cut them off from Blue Mtn. by a move out through Carrollton.

K. Garrard,
Brigadier-Gen., Commanding Division.

CSA
Hqtrs. Army of Tennessee,
Gadsden, Ala., Oct. 22, 1864.

Major-Gen. Joseph Wheeler,
Commanding Cavalry Corps:
General: ...You must endeavor to keep the Atlanta and Dalton railroad constantly cut, and should the enemy evacuate Atlanta you must destroy all the road north of the Chattahoochee, and constantly concentrating toward your left be prepared to join at any time the main body of the army...

A.P. Mason,
Major and Asst. Adjutant-Gen.

Hqtrs. Army of Tennessee,
Tuscumbia, Ala., October 30, 1864.

Major-Gen. Cobb:
Instead of moving directly against the works at Atlanta I suggest you move from Newnan against the railroad between the Chattahoochee and Etowah, if the necessary transportation can be obtained.

J. Hood,
General.

FED
Marietta, November 11, 1864.

Capt. L.M. Dayton,
Aide-de-Camp:
Four deserters came in this morning; left Montgomery on 2nd; came to Opelika on cars; left that place on 4th; passed Carrollton on 9th. Hood was at Corinth. All convalescent soldiers now being sent to that point. Some infantry and 1,500 cavalry at Opelika. Three brigades of cavalry at Carrollton, and five regiments at Villa Rica. Small force at West Point and Newnan. Cars run to Newnan. No information regarding Atlanta and Macon railroad. Citizens from Carrollton, and other points in that direction, think we are retreating from Atlanta.

J. Kilpatrick,
Brigadier-Gen.

BIBLIOGRAPHY

1916 Albert, Alphaeus H. RECORD OF AMERICAN UNIFORM AND HISORICAL BUTTONS, Byerstown Publishing Co., Byerstown, Pa.

1998 Atlanta Regional Commission, CHATTAHOOCHEE RIVER FROM PEACHTREE CREEK TO WEST POINT LAKE CORRIDOR PLAN STUDY, ARC, Atlanta, Ga.

1929 Baggett, Helen Dorsett, HOMESPUN, unpublished, 400 pages. A manuscript at the Old Campbell County Courthouse, in Fairburn, which relates one woman's experience crossing the battle area between near present Douglasville and Campbellton.

1908 Barron, S.B., THE LONE STAR DEFENDERS, Neale Publishing Co., N. Y. and Washington, D.C.

1976 Bowen, William and Linda F. Carnes, METAL DETECTION AS A TECHNIQUE IN URBAN ARCHEOLOGICAL SURVEY: A PRELIMINARY STATE.MENT, Early Georgia Vol. 4, The Society for Georgia Archeology, Athens, Ga. I had the pleasure of working with Bowen and Carnes on the eastern extension of the Marta Rail System. The vast areas to be studied and the historical nature of the east metro area led to experimenting with metal detectors.

1891 Davis, Major George B., Mr. Leslie J. Perry and Mr. Joseph W. Kirkley, Board of Publication, THE WAR OR THE REBELLION: A Compilation of the Official Records of the Union and Confederate Armies, GPO Washington, D.C. This is in seven parts of a 170 volumes of the official papers of both armies. The Atlanta Campaign was covered in Volumes 38 and 39, including 7 sections. The most recent reprints are seven volume sets.

DIARY OF LT. PANKEY, FIRST KENTUCKY CAVALRY, Unpublished, in the care of The Daughters of the Confederacy, Douglas County.

1993 Dickey, Thomas S. and Peter C. George, FIELD ARTILLERY PROJECTILES OF THE AMERICAN CIVIL WAR, Arsenal Publications, Mechanicsville, Va.

1979 Dyer, Fredrick H., A COMPENDIUM OF THE WAR OF THE REBELLION. Vol 2, Morningside, Dayton, Ohio.

1894 Eastham, Tarrant, THE WILD RIDERS OF THE FIRST KENTUCKY CAVALRY, R.H.Caruthers, Louisville, Ky.

1996 Evans, David, SHERMAN'S HORSEMEN: UNION CAVALRY OPERATIONS IN THE ATLANTA CAMPAIGN, Indiana University Press, Bloomington and Indianapolis.

1976 FIGHTING WITH ROSS' TEXAS CAVALRY BRIGADE, CSA: DIARY OF LT. GEORGE L. GRISSOM, ADJ., NINTH TEXAS CAVALRY, Hill, Jr. College Press, Hillsboro, Texas.

1993 Hale, Douglas, THE THIRD TEXAS CAVALRY IN THE CIVIL WAR, University of Oklahoma Press, Norman, Oklahoma.

2003 Henderson, Ray, ANNEEWAKEE TRAILS: A SITE REPORT, Douglas County Archeology Association.

1995 Henderson, Ray, THE CIVIL WAR ON THE LOWER SWEET WATER CREEK BASIN, Lillium Press, Douglasville, Ga.

1996 Henderson, Ray, A SELF-GUIDED DRIVING TOUR OF HISTORIC SITES IN DOUGLAS COUNTY, The Douglas County Historic Commission.

1896 HISTORY OF THE FIRST REGIMENT OF TENNESSEE VOLUNTEER CAVALRY IN THE GREAT WAR OF THE REBELLION, W.R. Carter and Co., Knoxville, Tenn.

1991 Howell, H.Grady, Jr., TO LIVE AND DIE IN DIXIE, HISTORY OF THE THIRD MISSISSIPPI INFANTRY, Chickasaw Bayou Press, Jackson, Miss.

1991 Kirkland, Turner, DIXIE GUN WORKS, INC., Dixie Gun Works, Union City, Tenn.

1975 Krakow, Kenneth K., GEORGIA PLACENAMES, Winship Press, Macon, Ga.

1993 Lane, Mills B., TIMES THAT PROVED PEOPLE'S PRINCIPLES, Beehive Press, Savannah.

1963 Lord, Frances A., CIVIL WAR COLLECTOR'S ENCYCLOPEDIA, Castle, Seacausus, N.J.

1980 McKee, W. Reid and M.E. Mason, Jr., CIVIL WAR PROJECTILES II: SMALL ARMS AND FIELD ARTILLERY, Rapidan Press, Mechanicsville, Virginia.

1994 Melton, Jack, Jr. and Lawrence E. Pawl, INTRODUCTION TO FIELD ARTILLERY ORDINANCE, 1861-1865, Kennesaw Mountain Press, Kennesaw, Ga.

1984 McGuinn, William F. and Bruce S. Bazelon, AMERICAN MILITARY BUTTON MAKERS AND DEALERS: MFR.BACKMARKS AND DATES, Wllliam F. McGuinn, Maclean, Va.

1901 Montgomery, Frank A.: REMINISCENCES OF A MISSISSIPPIAN IN THE CIVIL WAR, Cincinnati, Robert Clarke Company Press.

1991 Mullinax, Steven E., CONFEDERATE BELT BUCKLES AND PLATES, Odonnell Publications, Alexandria, Va.

1993 OLD CAMPBELL COUNTY, GA.: LAND DEED RECORDS 1828-1854, W.H. Wolfe and Associates, Roswell, Ga.

1885 Smith, Daniel P., COMPANY K, FIRST ALABAMA REGIMENT, by Survivors, Prattville, Ala.

1993 THE STORY OF THE FIFTY FIFTH REGIMENT, ILLINOIS VOLUNTEER INFANTRY IN THE CIVIL WAR, 1861-65. Blue Acorn Press, Huntington, W. Va.

1975 YANKEE ARTILLERY: THROUGH THE CIVIL WAR WITH ELI LILLY'S INDIANA BATTERY, University of Tennessee Press, Knoxville

1985 Yeoman, R.S., A GUIDEBOOK OF U.S. COINS, Western Publishing Co., Racine, Wisconsin.